A Sea-Dog of Devon

A Life of Sir John Hawkins, English Naval Commander, Privateer and Slaver of the 16th Century

By R. A. J. Walling

Published by Pantianos Classics

ISBN-13: 978-1-78987-268-2

First published in 1907

Sir John Hawkins

(From an original oil painting in the possession of Miss Mary W. S. Hawkins, at Hayford Hall, Buckfastleigh, Devon.)

Contents

Introduction vi

Chapter I - The Age 8

Chapter II - The Family of Hawkins 15

Chapter III - The Youth of John Hawkins 20

Chapter IV - The Trade in Negro Slaves 24

Chapter V - Second Voyage to the West Indies 31

Chapter VI - On the Spanish Main 37

Chapter VII - The Return to England 43

Chapter VIII - The Affair of San Juan 50

Chapter IX - The Affair of San Juan *(continued)* 56

Chapter X - The Affair of San Juan *(concluded)* 63

Chapter XI - Aftermath 70

Chapter XII - The Feria Plot 74

Chapter XIII - The Favour of the Queen 81

Chapter XIV - Elizabeth's Board of Admiralty 86

Chapter XV - An Admiralty Memorandum 94

Chapter XVI - The Armada 99

Chapter XVII - The Fight with the Santa Anna 105

Chapter XVIII - Figures 110

Chapter XIX - The Dainty 116

Chapter XX - The Bitter End 121

Chapter XXI - Characteristics 128

Notes 132

A. — The Family of Hawkins 132

B. — Authorities 133

C. — Hawkins and the Admiralty 133

Introduction

The author of this book has rightly placed John Hawkins among the first of those to whose undaunted spirit our sea supremacy is due. With Drake and Raleigh, the Gilberts and John Davis, Hawkins was among the greatest and most resolute of those famous men of Devon who made the earliest expeditions to the unknown shores of the New World. Less bold and generous in temperament, perhaps, than Drake, less gifted as a statesman than Raleigh, without the inspiration of Humphrey Gilbert, Raleigh's half-brother, but with the attractive qualities of John Davis — Hawkins deserved well of his country. He was a man of courage and resource. He possessed in a high degree administrative ability. He was a leader in an age of splendid achievements. He deserves to be better known to his countrymen in these days.

In introducing the present vigorous narrative to the reader, we shall endeavour briefly to describe the circumstances and the prevailing views of the age in which Hawkins lived. It is necessary to take account of environments in estimating character and conduct. The author undertakes to vindicate his hero from the charge of having inaugurated our British slave trade. Those who have made this reproach against Hawkins confuse the ideals of the nineteenth or twentieth century with those of the sixteenth. The great captain acted in conformity with the spirit of his age. The Portuguese and Spaniards had engaged without scruple in the slave trade. Prince Henry of Portugal, the so-called navigator, and King John II. combined zeal for the saving of the souls of negroes with a recognition of the possibility of profiting by the labour of their bodies.

We are brought to another point which those who read the life of those valiant English seamen should bear in mind. Our great navigators — bold, enterprising, and resolute as they were — came late into the field. Both the Portuguese and the Spaniards were before us. The courageous Portuguese captains who gradually pushed along the coasts of Africa, until Bartholomew Diaz doubled the Cape of Good Hope and Vasco da Gama reached India by sea, were the pioneers of the expeditions of our East India merchants. The voyages of Columbus, the exploration of Nicuesa and Ojeda, and the supreme triumph of Vasco Nuñez de Balboa, "the man who knew not when he was beaten," the first of white men to look upon the Pacific, revealed an El Dorado from which gold poured into the coffers of Spain. Their success stirred up the spirit of enterprise. Bold hearts in every maritime country were eager to share the spoil. The Spaniards were not willing that others should have part in the advantages of trade with the newly discovered lands. Their exclusive policy led inevitably to smuggling. The measures of repression which they adopted provoked sanguinary reprisals. Hawkins and Drake were overwhelmed in the treacherous affair at San Juan de Ulloa, and barely escaped with their lives. They resolved to take vengeance, the one by subtlety, and the other by the capture of Nombre de Dios, the sacking of Vera Cruz, and the seizing of the wealth of the silver-laden mules of Spain.

Peace could be no longer maintained. There followed the fierce struggle of 1588, in which Englishmen were proved to be the finest seamen in Europe. The Spaniards, though they had done so much to open up the New World, as seamen were not the equals of Englishmen. They were largely dependent on the skill of the navigators of Genoa and other parts of Italy. It is interesting to note that it was largely through the translation, in 1555, by Richard Eden, of the "Decades" of Peter Martyr, descriptive of Spanish and Portuguese expeditions, and in part through his rendering from the Spanish in the following year of Martin Cortes's "Arte de Navigar," published at Seville, that the voyages of our seamen were made more easy, and the first knowledge was gained of the wealth which might be acquired in the New World.

To sum up, John Hawkins is one of an illustrious band of navigators, English and foreign, to whom the opening up of trade with America is due. His professional attainments were high. He was master in seamanship, and in the art of the shipbuilder. His services were brilliant. He took a leading part in the fierce struggle with the Spaniards. In the interests of religion, and from a selfish desire to secure the monopoly in a valuable trade, they had sought to enclose the New World and bar the way to the Indies. English seamen and merchants were resolved that the barriers should be broken down.

In the volume here presented the fine career of John Hawkins is described in a deeply interesting narrative. The biography of such a man is full of instruction, and necessarily embraces a general survey of the great age in which he lived.

BRASSEY

JOHN LEYLAND

Chapter I - The Age

On a September day of the year 1568, amid the reek of powder smoke, the roar of culverins, and the cries of wounded men between the decks of the ship *Jesus of Lubek,* a Sea Dog of Devon was athirst. He made a gallant figure in gay attire, for he had just risen from his courtly entertaining of a grandee of Spain. Cheering on of gunners against great odds, breathing of vengeance against a ghastly treachery, inhaling the smother of war in the tropical air of Mexico — this was thirsty work.

"He called to Samuel his page for a cup of beer," says the quaint Chronicler, "who brought it to him in a silver cup. And he, drinking to all the men, willed the gunners to stand by their ordnance lustily, like men. He had no sooner set the cup out of his hand but a demi-culverin struck away the cup and a cooper's plane that stood by the mainmast, and ran out on the other side of the ship; which nothing dismayed our general, for he ceased not to encourage us..."

If it be true that, in the moment when Death breathes upon the face of a man as he passes by, the man has vision of his life as in the flash of magic crystal, never doubt that the wind of the culverin shot cleared for an instant the red mist of battle and disclosed to John Hawkins the garden of a gabled house in Plymouth. There he saw two boys at play, their game disturbed by the coming of mariners fresh from far seas, their game forgotten as they hung upon the converse of those sailors with their father of the perils and rewards of daring men who furrowed uncharted seas in the golden west. There he saw himself, one of those wide-eyed boys, flush and thrill as the microcosm of his life was suddenly revealed — glittering with shining adventure, red with the hue of war, dark with the shades of intrigue, following the star of high emprise. The boy who had stood in the garden at Plymouth was on the deck of his flagship in San Juan de Ulloa, the thunder of disastrous battle was around him, the powder smoke thickened again.

"He ceased not to encourage us, saying, ' Fear nothing, for God, who hath preserved me from this shot, will also deliver us from these traitors and villains.'"

"Fear nothing" is the keynote of Hawkins's career. "God...will deliver us!" comprehends his simple philosophy. This prototype of the Sea Dogs has been unaccountably overshadowed in the general literature of the Spanish raids and the Armada time by Drake. The tremendously romantic figure of Sir Francis has obsessed the public imagination, almost to the exclusion of equally important figures among his contemporaries. There is something almost uncanny about the fascination that Drake exercised over the men of his time, and the influence of the Drake legends has persisted to our own day.

"The Captain" he was called by the people of Plymouth; the Spaniards believed him to be assisted by the infernal powers in his prodigious exploits against them. His story has become encrusted with supernatural growths: he threw chips of wood into the sea, and they sprang up stately ships of war armed and equipped at all points; he magically brought water from Dartmoor to Plymouth in a time of drought by uttering an incantation, whereupon the stream followed his horse's hoofs from the uplands to the town. There is the legend of Drake's Drum, with which all readers of Mr. Corbett and Mr. Newbolt are familiar. I have no purpose to depreciate Drake, the Admirable Crichton of the Sixteenth Century seamen. He was a great leader and a great commander, and his influence upon the naval history of his time, and his place in the history of the world, are in no manner of question. Yet it is impossible to resist the conclusion that the almost exclusive attention given to him in the modern revival of interest in the Tudor Navy has pushed into the background many other men of large pattern, and greatest among them John Hawkins.

John Hawkins was much more than mariner; but he was mariner first and other things after. This not only in point of time; his other notable qualities and acquirements arose out of his quality and acquirement as mariner. If he became soldier, it was because maritime adventure imposed the necessity upon him. If he became diplomatist, it was to complete work begun at sea. If he became statesman, it was to administer the naval affairs of England. Wherever he was, in whatever complicated course he found himself at any time in his career, his thoughts were at sea, he dreamed of blue water, and longed to exchange the cloak of the courtier for the uniform of the captain, or the pedestal of high office for his own quarter-deck.

The life of John Hawkins is written in a hundred books: he is in the background of every naval history of the sixteenth century; but he has never yet had a biographer. If this is not actually by way of being a reproach to his country, it is at least something strange that so striking a figure in the English school of action should have lacked a literary portrait. Within the limits assigned to this volume a complete biography is impossible; if, however, there should arise from these pages a suggestion towards a detailed "Life," they will have served a good purpose.

It has been said that modern English character was moulded in the Reformation. It is a comprehensive, but a true saying. To the national movement of the sixteenth century we owe not a little of our modern greatness, our naval position, our world-empire. Only one facet of this thought need be examined here. The Reformation was the beginning of England's "glorious isolation," and the inspiration of the great sea-conflict with the Catholic Power. The wax of the systems lasted till 1688, and in the sense that the Reformation was not complete till William and Mary signed the Declaration of Rights, the national character and destinies did not emerge from the crucible till another century had passed. But the sixteenth century struggle with Spain determined a great deal when it determined the naval supremacy of England; it cultivated the maritime genius of the Islanders, and laid the foundations of our colonial and imperial system in West and East. The model of English seamanship was cast; to the Spanish wars we look for the earliest precedents of modern naval traditions. How great a part the Hawkinses played in the making of the Navy, the establishment of seamanlike traditions, and the extension of the British Power in distant latitudes it will be the essay of these pages to demonstrate.

We must go back to the reign of Henry VIII. to find the genesis of the Hawkins family's connection with the Navy; and, as it was Henry VIII. who began the work of naval organisation in the modern sense, they may be said to have had their part in the creation of the British Navy as a fighting machine. Dockyards were first provided in this reign at Deptford — scene of much of Sir John's work later on — Woolwich, and Portsmouth; commissioners were first appointed to look after the financial affairs of the maritime forces; and the status and pay of Admirals, Vice-Admirals, and inferior officers were settled. The naval spirit came into being. England assumed the sovereignty of the Northern seas, and the nation began to feel that its mission in the world was greater than to populate and administer these small islands. The ambition of maritime discovery was lively; the need for an efficient naval force, not merely to prevent invasion of the homeland, but also to afford protection to the ever-widening interests of British commerce, began to be felt; the modern naval policy was born.

Though under Edward and Mary the tendency was rather to reduce than to increase Henry's naval force of 12,000 tons and 8,000 men, even in the reign of the Catholic Queen the maritime prestige of England was jealously upheld. We come across a curious incident of naval etiquette during the voyage of Philip to this country to espouse the Queen. The English Lord High Admiral compelled Philip to strike the flag he was flying at his main topmast-head in homage to the flag of England. How nauseating such a performance must have been to the proud stomach of Philip we may imagine; the Spanish Admiral did not accede to the demand until a shot had been fired into him. Then he saw the force of the argument. Even when the Admiral had struck, English *amour propre* was not satisfied. The whole of the Spanish fleet of 160 vessels must strike flags and lower topsails; and this was done before the British ships received order to salute. We have in this a precedent for action taken in later years by Sir John Hawkins himself. The story is quaintly told by Sir Richard, his son. The date is 1567, and the place Plymouth Harbour: —

"There came a fleete of Spaniards of aboue fiftie sayle of shippes, bound for Flaunders, to fetch the queen donna Anna de Austria, last wife to Philip the second of Spaine, which entred betwixt the iland and the maine, without vayling their top-sayles, or taking in of their flags: which my father Sir John Hawkins, (admirall of a fleete of her majesties shippes, then ryding in Cattwater), perceiving, commanded his gunner to shoote at the flag of the admirall, that they might thereby see their error: which, notwithstanding, they persevered arrogantly to keepe displayed; whereupon the gunner at the next shott, lact the admirall through and through, whereby the Spaniards finding that the matter beganne to grow to earnest took in their flags and top-sayles, and so ranne to an anchor.

"The generall presently sent his boat, with a principal personage to expostulate the cause and reason of that proceeding; but my father would not permit him to come into his ship, nor to heare his message; but by another Gentleman commanded him to returne, and to tell his general, that in as much as in the queenes port and chamber, he had neglected to do the acknowledgment and reverence which all owe unto her majestie (especially her ships being present), and comming with so great a navie, he could not but give suspetion by such proceeding of malicious intention, and therefore required him, that within twelve hours he should depart the port, upon paine to be held as a common enemy, and to proceed against him with force."

This dispute was in the end adjusted without any such extreme measures; the Spaniard acknowledged himself to be in fault, and the proceedings concluded with "the auncient amities renewed, by feasting each other aboord and ashore." The temper of the incident is significant of the British determination thus early that no Power, however great and aggressive, should be allowed to assume an overlordship of the seas. It took a long time to convince Philip that the English meant what these things implied; "Achines de Plimua," as Hawkins was called in Spain, had to raid him here and there to assert the right of free commerce for Englishmen; Drake had to singe his beard in the harbour of Cadiz; Howard, Hawkins, Drake, and the rest, had to scatter and destroy his mighty Armada before the truth was borne in upon him.

Perfect daring, the supreme self-confidence that comes of faith in a national cause and complete knowledge of the means by which it may be best promoted — these were the characteristics of the great seamen of Queen Elizabeth. But these qualities in their highest manifestation — seen in the achievements of Hawkins and his companions — were not the spontaneous creation of one generation; they were a heritage which the Elizabethans developed as we know how. It was not until the end of the fifteenth century that the English gave their minds to maritime discovery. The Wars of the Roses had been too absorbing and exhausting to permit of any external enterprise. But the era of internal peace that was inaugurated with the Tudors liberated a tremendous force of character and gallantry, which soon began to expend itself in sea-adventures. British seamen followed the Portuguese into distant seas, and ere a century had passed they had outstripped all predecessors and competitors in the boldness of their designs and the glory of their achievements.

A great deal of the work of expansion, conquest, and discovery was done by adventurers whose connection with the national Navy was loose enough; so far as the Hawkinses were concerned, though they came to the front in the first instance as merchant adventurers and the patrons of privateers, their association with the Navy was close. In those days of Henry VIII, when, as already set out, the real foundations of the modern Navy system were laid, the first Hawkins who takes rank as a great seaman was an officer of the Navy. His son John became the great "admirall" and Treasurer of the Navy; his grandson Richard also attained the highest naval rank. They were all distinguished scions of the great race of Plymouth seamen. They were adventurers, but much more; they were merchants whose genius and industry raised their fortunes so that of their wealth they could supply what the parsimony of their sovereign left lacking on occasions; they could share in the greatest financial enterprises of their time. They were daring sailors, but much more; they were, if not courtiers, yet skilled men in statecraft, and leaders commanding a devotion that amounted almost to idolatry. They were the epitome of the spirit of their age.

What that spirit was may be read in the eloquent words of Froude. It was the spirit of liberty, of independence, of freedom; the world was opening wide before Englishmen; the ocean-sea was giving up to them its remotest secrets. That which stood between them and the fairest prospects that the earth could offer was the power of Spain; that power it was which also menaced their civil and religious liberties at home. It was Spain that intrigued with Mary Queen of Scots and stirred up rebellion in Ireland; it was Spain that threw English seamen and traders into the prisons of the Inquisition, starved and tortured them, or burned them at the stake. The story of the illicit war on the Spanish possessions, preceding the licit war that culminated in the Armada, is the story of a nation's great uprising and outcry against the pretensions of "Popish tyranny" and Spanish Imperialism. The leaders and the spokesmen were the seamen of the West. In the Western seas, in the Spanish ports, they took their price for the massacres of Smithfield, for the horrors to which their brothers and friends had been subjected in Spanish prisons; they damaged the possessions and harassed the subjects of the State which was their nation's enemy; they began the long process of destroying the proud, vainglorious power of Spain.

It is not to be pretended that altruistic motives, or even patriotism, alone ruled the conduct of the adventurers of the West. Their imagination was fired by hope of rich reward for those who would dare venture; plunder played its part in their endeavours; the love of adventure for adventure's sake was also potent. Some facts and many fictions were circulated in England relating to the wealth the Spaniards derived from their possessions in the West Indies and on the Pacific Coast; El Dorado beckoned. These excited the desires of merchants, speculators and soldiers of fortune. But any impartial reading of the original papers of the time, written by the sailors themselves or their chroniclers, must convince that to regard them as mere buccaneers and pirates is to entertain a sorry misconception. A great deal of the work done by the Hawkinses, for instance, was in the nature of perfectly fair trading, and would do no shame to honest merchants and ship owners of our day. And so far as the spoiling of Spanish ships and the capture of Spanish treasure was concerned, it is to be remembered that Spain was The Enemy, and that these men fully believed themselves to be serving God and their

Queen what time they also helped themselves to the contents of Philip's galleons. They did unto Philip as they knew Philip would do unto them if he might.

In any estimate of the events of this period, the fact must be constantly kept in view that the warfare between the English privateers — whether equipped with the Royal assistance and consent or not — and the Spaniards was but emblematic of the greater conflict between the two systems striving for mastery on the continent of Europe. If a blow could be struck in any part of the world at a Spanish ship, it was a blow at the Arch-Enemy, a blow at the Catholic system, a blow at the Power which would have imposed the Inquisition on the whole world. English seamen knew the Inquisition, how relentlessly it struck down the unhappy Protestant who got within its reach. "It was not necessary that a poor sailor should have been found teaching heresy. It was enough if he had an English Bible and Prayer Book with him in his kit; and stories would come into Dartmouth or Plymouth how some lad that everybody knew — Bill or Jack or Tom, who had wife or father or mother among them, perhaps — had been seized hold of for no other crime, been flung into a dungeon, tortured, starved, set to work in the galleys, or burned in a fool's coat, as they called it, at an *auto-de-fé* at Seville." [1] Galleons burning to the water's edge, rifled treasuries of Spanish gold, fierce fights at sea, raids on Spanish colonial towns — these made answer to the *auto-de-fé*; and a man of Plymouth or Dartmouth sailed into the powder murk with no less heart because of the fate of Bill or Jack or Tom whom he had known in the High Street or the Butterwalk, or had accompanied to St. Andrew's or St. Saviour's, or had joined in dance and carouse at the Midsummer Night's Wake.

Who shall doubt the sincerity of a man like John Hawkins when, writing to Burleigh, he says: "I have briefly considered upon a substantial course and the material reasons that by mine own experience I know (with God's assistance) will strongly annoy and offend the King of Spain, the mortal enemy of our religion and the present government of the realm of England" [2] Hawkins was no sniveller, no hypocrite; when he invoked the Divine assistance for a project of annoying and offending Philip as the mortal enemy of the English church and nation, he believed that he would get it, and acted in that belief. It is time to destroy the impression that the seamen out of the West were no better than pirates and corsairs, and that their only motive was plunder. They were devout and God-fearing men in their fashion, and they made no doubt that their warfare was religious as well as political and personal. Hawkins's sailing orders to his crews in 1564 form no bad rule of conduct: "Serve God daily; love one another; preserve your victuals; beware of fire; and keep good company."

To come even closer to this question of the morality of the plunder accomplished on the high seas, the case must be judged by the ruling ethic of the age; and the privateers had fair precedent for everything they did in the notorious instance of the Genoese ducats. It was in 1568 that Philip, pressed by the necessities of the war in the Netherlands, borrowed half a million sterling from two banking-houses of Genoa. The money, despatched by several ships, was to be delivered to the Duke of Alva at Antwerp. The privateers of the Channel, with their headquarters at Plymouth, obtained information of the approach of the treasure-ships, gave chase to them, and drove them to various harbours for shelter, so that Alva's war-chest, instead of arriving safely at Antwerp, was distributed in the ports of Plymouth, Southampton, and Fowey. One of the vessels, commanded by Capitan Diaz, sailed into a hornets' nest in Plymouth Sound, where were numerous ships of the Prince of Conde's private fleet and English vessels flying his flag. William Hawkins, mayor of the town, brother of John Hawkins, was awaiting the arrival of the latter from San Juan de Ulloa. [3] The Spaniards under Diaz knew all about the treachery proposed, if not of the actual disaster that had befallen Hawkins; and the Spanish captain was naturally anxious to prevent the news from reaching Plymouth's ears. He therefore made up a cock-and-bull story for local consumption to the effect that John Hawkins's expedition had been completely successful, and that he was returning laden with fabulous riches; "the worst boy in those ships might be a captain for riches."

Unfortunately for Senor Diaz, not long after his own arrival came the veritable news of San Juan; and English indignation vented itself upon him and his treasure. William Hawkins implored permission to make war on the ducats that Diaz carried in order that he might himself be recompensed for his losses in the ill-fated expedition. He did not get it, but the government landed the money and conveyed it to London by road. There the agent of the Genoese bankers found that Queen Elizabeth's security was better than King Philip's, and decided to lend it to the English government. Consequently, half the wealth designed to assist in the shedding of Protestant blood in the Low Countries was sent to the Protestant Prince of Orange, and the other half went to the support of the Protestant Queen Elizabeth's Navy.

It is a curious attitude of mind that questions the wisdom of such a proceeding. True, England was not now nominally at war with Spain, but the conditions of war existed very completely in everything but name, and the name itself was added at the very end of the contest a few years later. The English people were certainly at war with Spain, and the systems represented by Philip and Elizabeth were in the throes of a struggle for life and death. Without the seamanship, the bravery, the daring of the privateers, without the experience they had gained in all parts of the Western world, it is not unlikely that the history of 1588 might have read very differently, and the Great Deliverance would have been impossible. Men must be judged by the light of their age; England, judging the sea-dogs of Elizabeth by the light of the sixteenth century, has approved them brave patriots and dauntless heroes, and enshrined them in imperishable memory.

[1] Froude: "English Seamen."
[2] Hawkins to Lord Burleigh. State Papers.
[3] See Chapter IX.

Chapter II - The Family of Hawkins

"Old Master William Hawkyns," as Hakluyt calls him, father of Sir John, was a great sea captain who in 1513 was probably master of *The Great Galley,* second ship in Henry's Navy. In later years his seamanlike skill, his knowledge of the world, his adventurous disposition, and his genius for business obtained for him the distinguished favour of bluff King Hal. It is not possible to ascertain just how the friendship between the sovereign and the Plymouth sailor grew up. "King Harry loved a man," quotes Froude; and adds: "He knew a man when he saw one. He made acquaintance with sea-captains at Portsmouth and Southampton. In some way or other he came to know one Mr. William Hawkins, of Plymouth, and held him in especial esteem." But we can hardly be in doubt that it was through his qualities and reputation as a seaman that Hawkins's acquaintance with the King came about; those fine qualities and that high reputation certainly preserved him in the royal favour thereafter.

By trading and adventuring he acquired a large fortune. He was the owner of a considerable property in Plymouth, and is described as one of the richest men, if not actually the richest man, in the town. In the earliest list in existence of freemen of the old borough, he standsfifth on the roll. He was "Receiver" in the year 1524-5, and, in the later years of his life, was twice mayor. Mr. Worth, who examined the records of the Corporation minutely, thought that in all probability he was admitted a freeman in the early years of the century. He became member of Parliament for Plymouth, and for discharging his duties as a representative he was paid the sum of sixteen pence a day. Elsewhere in the books of the Corporation, he is mentioned as having been conspicuous in 1527-8 in "manning the bulwarks to defend the argosy against the Frenchmen." The exact record of this incident is as follows: —

"Item received of tharrogosye for defending their shippe against the ffrenshemen that would have taken her, xvjli xivs ivd,"

"Tharrogosye" was "the argosy" — probably a Spanish merchant vessel attacked by the French — and the £16 14s. 4d. was compensation for the part taken by the men of Plymouth in saving her from capture. At this time, it may be noted, the English were hand in glove with the nation destined to be their bitterest foe fifty years later. The Reformation proper had not begun, and Henry VIII. and Charles V. were leagued together against France.

Now, before he had come into national prominence, William Hawkins was a noteworthy person on his native heath, a capitalist who could lend money to the Corporation, or purchase supplies for them, and afford to wait for repayment by instalments. Thus, in 1529 he sold to the town 196 lbs. of gunpowder and two brass guns. The gunpowder was taken at the price of 6d. per lb., and the total debt was repaid by the Corporation in three annual instalments of £8. Six years afterwards he lent cash to the borough Fathers, which was paid back in annuities of £4 a year. Earlier than this, Hawkins had begun the three voyages on which his historical fame as a seaman rests. The first of them may be fixed about the year 1528. Mention has already been given to the fact that, on the liberation of English enterprise after the Wars of the Roses, the thoughts of men were turned to new lands of promise and English began to follow Portuguese and Spanish adventurers over the Western Ocean. The voyages performed in the reign of Henry VII. were not organised by Englishmen. As Froude says: —

"Columbus had offered the New World to Henry VII. while the discovery was still in the air. He had sent his brother to England with maps and globes, and quotations from Plato to prove its existence. Henry, like a practical Englishman, treated it as a wild dream. The dream had come from the gate of horn. America was found, and the Spaniard, and not the English, came into first possession of it. Still, America was a large place, and John Cabot, the Venetian, with his son Sebastian, tried Henry again. England might still be able to secure a slice. This time Henry VII. listened. Two small ships were fitted out at Bristol, crossed the Atlantic, discovered Newfoundland, coasted down to Florida, looking for a passage to Cathay, but could not find one. The elder Cabot died; the younger came home. The expedition failed, and no interest had been roused." [1]

It remained for Henry VIII. and William Hawkins to wake interest and tempt Englishmen to reach for the prizes that awaited their arrival in the far-off seas. Sebastian Cabot made another voyage to the River Plate in 1527, sent forth by Spanish merchants who intended that the ships should go to the Moluccas. The English had some hand in this expedition, for we are told by Robert Thorne — a Plymouth man, like Hawkins — that he and his partners advanced 1,400 ducats mainly in order that two friends of his who were "learned in cosmographie" should go in the ships and report to him on the country visited and obtain such useful knowledge as they could pick up about the navigation of those seas. It is to be remarked, however, that the first purely English expedition to the American continent was taken out by William Hawkins; further, that it was organised and equipped by him, and was his own private adventure. This was the voyage of 1528. Hakluyt, in introducing his account of it, remarks that Hawkins, "a man for his wisedom, valure, experience, and skill in sea causes much esteemed and beloued of K. Henry the 8, and being one of the principall Sea-captaines in the West parts of England in his time, not contented with the short voyages commonly made then onely to the knowne coaste of Europe, armed out a tall and goodlye shippe of his owne of the burthen of 250 tunnes called the *Paule of Plimmouth*." He adds that it was in this ship that Hawkins made "three long and famous voyages unto the coast of Brasil," and that such an enterprise was in those days very rare, "especially to our Nation."

The adventure led first to the Guinea Coast, and thus, curiously, set the precedent for the celebrated route adopted by John Hawkins in after times. The *Paule of Plimmouth* sailed into the mouth of the River Sestos, where Hawkins dropped anchor and began bartering with the natives and securing some of the profits that went to the building of the fortunes of the house. Ivory ("oliphant's teeth") and other commodities which the negroes had to dispose of were shipped into his vessel, and when his business was completed, he weighed and shaped a course to the West. The *Paule* was the first British ship that ever pushed a way into the waters of the Brazilian coast.

If William Hawkins had not been a great sailor and a great merchant, he would have been a statesman and a diplomatist. No ambassador from one friendly Power to another could have acted with more tact and discretion than he did towards the native chiefs with whom he trafficked. In all his voyages to the West, he never encountered any serious hostility or trouble, sagacious old trader and prescient man that he was. He "behaved himself so wisely with those savage people that he grew into great familiarity and friendship with them." Hawkins was the first English commander the Indians of that region had seen; they liked him well, for he spoke them fairly and treated them justly. Having returned to Plymouth, settled the accounts of his expedition, and put his affairs in order, he sailed a second time in 1530. He was effusively welcomed by the people with whom he had dealt before, and, when he weighed again for home, had a unique cargo on board. It included not only the valuable produce of the country, but a veritable native prince, one of the chiefs of the Indian tribes inhabiting the Brazilian coastlands. This was the first savage chief imported into England.

Hawkins was something of a courtier, and he knew full well how keenly King Henry would appreciate the services of a man who should procure him such a novel lion for exhibition in London. For this reason he would be anxious to make the attempt. But it is no small tribute to his suavity and diplomacy that he was able to induce the chieftain to accompany him. Remember that Hawkins was the first Englishman they had known, that he had only visited the country once before, and that if the people had any prejudices at all about the character and motives of the white man, these were derived from their acquaintance with the Spaniards, of whose dealings with the native tribes we know somewhat. Hawkins's method was to be perfectly frank and open with them. Doubtless he told them something of the grandeur of England and the marvels that awaited their adventurous chief. He agreed to leave behind him a hostage, and the pledge he gave was one of his own townsmen, Martin Cockeram, of Plymouth. So the *Paule* sailed, the savage potentate was landed at Plymouth, and by Hawkins taken up to London, and presented to the King at Whitehall. He was lionised just as better and worse men have been lionised since. The King and all the nobility did not a little marvel at the sight of this first specimen of the aboriginal American brought into England; as Hakluyt observes, their wonderment was not without cause:

"For in his cheeks were holes made according to their savage manner, and therein small bones were planted, standing an inch out from the said holes: which, in his own country, was reputed for a great bravery. He Kad also another hole in his nether lip, wherein was set a precious stone about the bigness of a pea. All his apparel, behaviour, and gesture were very strange to the beholders."

The Brazilian remained in England a year, much fêted and the object of great public curiosity. Then Hawkins commenced the fulfilment of his engagement to restore him to his own land unharmed. But royal favours, feasting, and the life of a civilisation different from his own disagreed with the chief's constitution, and he died on the voyage back: "It fell out in the way that by the change of air and alteration of diet, the said savage King died at sea." Here was a crucial test of the impression which Hawkins's character had made upon his Brazilian friends. If he had not convinced them of his sincerity and honesty, Master Martin Cockeram would never have seen Plymouth any more. But Master Cockeram did get back to Plymouth, and lived there to a good old age. The Indians, "being fully persuaded of the honest dealing of our men with their prince," restored the hostage to Hawkins and filled up his ship with goods, with which he sailed home to Devon. He went once more to the Spanish Main two years later, and then settled down to the life of a burgess of Plymouth, a prosperous merchant, and a popular Parliament man. He came back from his last voyage laden with the wealth of the Indies, and cloaked with the mysterious glory of an adventurer into the new world of the West. He was immediately elected Mayor of Plymouth.

When next he held that office the situation was altered. The Reformation was in full swing. The crusade against the ecclesiastical establishments had been set moving, and they had commenced pulling down the images in the churches and confiscating the parochial plate and valuables. "The Pious and Godly Institution of a Christian Man" had been compiled, the "monasteries had been suppressed, and the Abbeys had been rifled — among them those of Tavistock and Plympton, close home — Becket had been unsainted: the plate and jewels of the mother church of Plymouth, St. Andrew's, shared the fate of all the rest. The sympathies of Plymouth were Puritan from early times, and at the commencement of the Reformation it gave earnest of what it would do in another hundred years, when it was to make so great a fight on behalf of the Parliament against the Crown. It entered with zeal into the new movement, and became the headquarters of Huguenot privateers in the Channel.

William Hawkins, the leader of Plymouth men during his life, was the guiding spirit in the new movement, and it was with no mean satisfaction that he, as Mayor, received on behalf of the Corporation in 1540 the "church juells and other thynges," and made arrangements for their sale in London. In 1543 a still larger quantity of church furniture was handed to him, "to by therewith for the Toune gunpowder bowys and for arowys." During one of his visits to the capital in the capacity of member of Parliament he made these purchases — ten barrels of gunpowder, twenty bows, and thirty sheaves of arrows. His wealth and consequence continued to increase. In 1544 he bought the Manor of Sutton Vawter — the estate remained in the hands of the family for a century — and became the owner of other property in the town. In 1553, the year in which he had been re-elected to Parliament, the old man died.

It has seemed well to recite these details of a fine, active, useful life — a life full-blooded with the stream of enterprise that upsprang in the midst of the sixteenth century — in order to show the nature of the stock from which Sir John Hawkins issued. "Old William Hawkins" — so called contemporaneously to distinguish him from his son William — was, in fact, the first, the patriarch, of the Sea Dogs of Devon. Now note the family into which he married. Sir John Trelawny, distinguished owner of a great Cornish name, was with Henry at the Battle of Agincourt in 1415. He displayed great bravery in the fight, and the King rewarded him with an addition to his coat of arms and a pension of £20 per annum. On a tablet over the West Gate of the town of Launceston were the arms of Henry V., with an effigy, and beneath a couplet graven —

> "He that will do aught for mee,
> Let hym love well Sir John Trelawnee."

The third son of Sir John was Roger Trelawny, afterwards of Brightorre; Roger's only daughter and heiress was Joan, and Joan Trelawny became wife of William Hawkins. In this way, the merchant and adventurer allied himself with a good family and acquired a large fortune at the same time. The marriage was blessed with two sons, the elder, William, named after his father, and the younger, John, after his grandfather. It is the latter whose career we are to follow.

It is impossible, however, to leave the first of the Plymouth captains without a sentence or two in tribute of admiration for his strong and sterling character. He was valiant in action and sage in counsel. He had the wisdom of the serpent and the gentleness of the dove. He lived a long and varied Hfe, and he brought to the training of his two sons all the manifold advantages that an experience of the world almost unique in his day could give him. He had been a war-commander in the very infancy of naval warfare with explosive weapons; he had smelt powder in actions against the French; he knew of the business of a merchant what the known world could tell him; he had seen lands and peoples on which his eyes were the first English eyes to gaze; he had taken a full share in the duties of the chief office of his native town; he was at home in the Court and in the Parliament House. No more versatile character appears till his own sons go forth. And in all the later years of his life, it is the sea that calls him: as he stands on his quays at Plymouth, or walks upon its cliffs, it is of the Brazils that he talks to the youths budding into manhood, and of his last voyage in the *Paule of Plimmouth*, completed when they were in infancy. And this is their inspiration. William is already a man of consideration, and, as his father's heir, will become a great ship-owner, whose cruisers will be a constant deadly menace to the King of Spain and his fleets. John is just of age, and will presently make voyages far surpassing anything his father has achieved, become the organiser of the English Navy, and help to defeat the Armada. And so, with a long record of duty well done, having founded a race that shall live as long as the sea-history of his land, the old man closes his eyes upon the glitter of the waters and passes to his grave.

[1] Froude: "English Seamen."

Chapter III - The Youth of John Hawkins

John Hawkins, born in 1532, has been described as Patriarch of the Sea-Rovers. Reasons have been set out why that proud title belongs of prior right to his father. In his gay response to the invitation of the sea — none can doubt that it was gay and gladsome, for if ever the world held a born sailor it was John Hawkins — he was but following in the wake of his sire, fulfilling the tradition established in the time of the *Paule of Plimmouth*. The craving for adventure, the desire for progress in the art of seamanship, the admixture of the craft of ambassador and statesman and courtier with that of sailor and warrior — the precedent for these was great and recent in the family that gathered in the old house in Kinterbury-street of Plymouth.

Those who know the Plymouth of to-day and haply are acquainted with the narrow, darksome, grimy, utilitarian lane of factories and poor houses that bears the ancient name, and occupies the site of the fair mansions and gardens once ranged along the slope overlooking the valley and harbour of Sutton, will have difficulty in conjuring up the scene it must have presented in the sixteenth century. A great deal of the older part of Plymouth which was fashionable when Hawkins and Drake walked its streets has so degenerated. The High Street, near by Kinterbury Street, and other thoroughfares have "come down" in a melancholy manner as the tide of business and wealth has spread inland. The old houses, or such of them as remain, are let out in flats to the poorest people, and there is no means of identifying the place where the house and garden stood that old William Hawkins bought in 1537. Of Kinterbury Street in an aesthetic sense the less said the better. But when the Hawkinses occupied that "tenement and garden in a certain venella on the east of Kinterbury Street," the condition of affairs was very different; this was suburban luxury, embowered in green. From the sloping garden the boys had a fine, inspiriting outlook over the eastern harbour of Plymouth, Sutton Pool, and the Cattewater, that sheltered, almost landlocked arm of the sea where their father's ships lay, where they were themselves to embark on many a memorable voyage.

Nor was it a far cry to The Hawe, as the Hoe was then called — signifying a height — the historic cliff where Drake is reputed to have been playing bowls in 1588 when news of the arrival of Philip's Armada was brought. There they would be in the exciting times of their youth, when the old men played their games and told their tales of danger faced and glory won, when ships were going and coming between Plymouth Sound and all the known oceans. There, with no huge breakwater intervening between them and the vision of the Channel, with no lighthouse upon the deadly reef of Eddystone, they looked out upon the wide sea and felt its fascination, and turned from it to the wrinkled faces and blue eyes of ancient mariners, and breathed the atmosphere, imbibed the intoxication, submitted to the spell of it. The great sea called them with command, that great sea which was to be the winding sheet of one of them; they felt its oneness with themselves, its harmony with the soul within them, these sailors born. Their destiny was written in their father's life, in the surroundings of their youth. Open-eyed, wide-eared boys, listening to the converse of the sea-captains who frequented their home, gathered inspiration and stimulus for the deeds which in after years were to make them famous.

In another and distant part of England was being reared in similar circumstances a boy upon whose history their own was to exercise a powerful influence. In 1544, when John Hawkins was twelve years of age, Francis Drake was born at Tavistock. He was a kinsman of the Hawkinses, who in former years had established connections with the little town on the moorland frontier. While William and John Hawkins were watching the great growth of private maritime enterprise at Plymouth, Francis Drake was witnessing the first great outburst of naval progress in England from the banks and boats of the Medway, and keeping also the company of sailormen and adventurers. His father had removed from Devon to Kent while he was yet very young. Some controversy has gathered about the question of the relationship between Drake and the Hawkinses; doubt has been cast even on its existence. It has been said to be improbable because Drake himself never told Camden anything about it. Not in itself a very convincing negative; further, we have documentary evidence in the affirmative, which is worth a lot more. In a letter from William Hawkins, reference is made to "our kinsman called Fransyes Dracke" — the occasion being that on which Hawkins sent the future hero of Cadiz to London to Sir William Cecil with news of the disaster at San Juan. Drake does not seem to have been associated with the men of Plymouth till a later period. His first sea employment was from the Medway, and it was not until he had reached the age of twenty-two that he joined John Hawkins in the Guinea trade. Still, there would probably have been communication between the families.

The memory of their father's last voyage to the Spanish Main was twenty years old when he died and the brothers came into the possession of his business, his ships, and his wealth. In the same year, William, of whom a few words now fall to be said, was admitted to the Freedom of Plymouth, so that he was already recognised as a man of consequence in his native town. He stepped at once into his father's place. Indeed, he soon far excelled the influence the old gentleman had wielded; it is not long before we find him held in such esteem that he is tacitly regarded as the governor of the port. It was an unofficial position, arising from the extent of his relations with the varied commerce of the place and the great importance of his shipping property. From the beginning — it was probably the natural accompaniment of his headship of the family — he paid much more attention to local affairs than did his brother John, and although he was a man of great sea-knowledge and experience, he seems never to have had quite so broad an outlook upon the world. We discover him concerned in obtaining the revised Town's Charter from Queen Elizabeth in 1561, and in the transfer of St. Nicholas' Island (now known as Drake's Island) to the Corporation, and from the Corporation to the Crown; and at a comparatively early age he filled the office of mayor. He largely increased the local status of the family. The quays that had been built or purchased by his father in Sutton Harbour were fixed by Act of Parliament in 1558 as the sole quays at which goods might be legally landed in Plymouth. His local importance appears to have tended a little in the direction of monopoly. There is, however, no evidence that he abused his trust, for he remained popular enough to be re-elected mayor, and he was occupying the civic chair in the year of the Armada.

William Hawkins's purely local activities and interests need not detain us; but one significant fact is to be observed. As an owner of ships in the port of Plymouth, he was one of the earliest organisers of the great fleet of privateers that now began the career of terrorisation from which Spain suffered for so many years. To his influence and encouragement was due the circumstance that the volunteer ships of the Prince of Condé made their headquarters at Plymouth. Old William Hawkins, his father, was an earnest and enthusiastic partisan of the Protestant Reformation. His heir was a burning Protestant, and took no small share in the historic conversion of Plymouth into a Puritan stronghold. And he was not merely a passive owner of vessels which made raids on Spanish ships and Catholic towns. He himself sailed to the Spanish Main in command of his own flotillas, and was in some sharp fighting at Porto Rico. He held a commission under the Prince of Condé. There is no need to repeat here the drama of the Genoese ducats in which he was one of the chief actors.

Long before this, John Hawkins had begun to acquire his reputation. It is a rather silly fashion to represent every man who became a great seaman and fighter in Elizabethan days as a sort of hybrid between a stage pirate and a modern coal-lumper; and Hawkins, because he was a bluff and blunt man, has suffered more than most of his contemporaries from this kind of fiction. In actual fact, he was well-educated and accomplished for his time, and lived in excellent style. Some of his dispatches show a sense of the effect of words, though he was an artist rather with tacks and sheets, with guns and money, than with the pen. His first great voyage was begun when he was at the age of thirty, in 1562; but before this, as we learn from Hayluyt, he had made several trips to Spain and Portugal and the Canary Islands. In the Spanish ports he had heard fascinating stories of the glamour and the wealth of the Western Islands, which led to his first expedition into those waters.

From his earliest years the seaman-genius of Hawkins had displayed itself. Seamanship was his greatest care as a youth; it became a fixed passion. He cultivated it by the best means he could procure. He read mathematics and studied navigation theoretically and practically, and gave early promise of the greatness that awaited him not only in exploration and pioneering adventure, but in maritime administration. He showed some capacity for affairs generally, and only two years later than his brother (1555) was admitted as freeman of Plymouth. He was then just twenty-three years of age, but had already entered upon his profession. This is demonstrated in a really curious way. There happened to be two John Hawkynses admitted freemen in the same year, and he is distinguished as "John Hawkyns, majynr." One can imagine no title which John Hawkins would have preferred to it, either at twenty-three or at sixty-three. He is registered in this year as the owner of the *Peter of Plymouth,* about which vessel it was declared that she had been captured by the French at sea before war was declared. Such complaint, we may take it, was not a very serious matter among men whose ideas of such international law as existed were, to say the least of it, loose.

Such a man as John Hawkins was, now achieving maturity, would be very unlikely to find content for his ambitions in sailing seas that were known, in prosaic voyages that everybody else had made to the ports of Europe and the western coast of Africa. The great world of the West was being opened up. The legends current about it could not fail to be attractive to a trader of adventurous disposition.

There was another stimulus which would be equally operative in the case of Hawkins. Henry VII. had been offered the chance of acquiring for the English everything that was meant by a first footing in the West Indies; he rejected the opportunity, and it was accepted by Spain. Spain did not intend, having won great territories and great riches there, to share its wealth with any other nation. The facts about the islands and their resources, and about the navigation of the waters of those regions, were therefore maintained in great secrecy. The Spaniards placed an embargo on trade between their settlers and the ships of other nations; they built a wall of exclusion. That was one of the prime factors in the initiation of John Hawkins's voyages. He saw that fame and profit were to be obtained in the West; above all he saw that the wall was there, and that it was not invulnerable to a man of ingenuity and strength. He possessed both in a very high degree. He had not made many voyages to the Canaries before he came to the determination that the breach could be made, and that he would be the man to make it. Here we have the origin of the first dispute between John Hawkins and Philip of Spain. On it hung momentous issues.

Chapter IV - The Trade in Negro Slaves

Up to 1562, Hawkins had been a simple trader. He had made a name as a skilful sea-captain, and had added largely to his wealth. But it had all been done by way of perfectly legitimate business, that is to say, he had not come into conflict with any of the peoples with whom he traded, and was no foe to their governments. In this eventful year, however, occurred the great departure. He had "made divers voyages to the Isles of the Canaries, and...by his good and upright dealing...grown in love and favour with the people." [1] It was here he found the immediate inspiration of his great adventures. The little archipelago was intimately associated with the great explorations of the fifteenth century. Hence Columbus jumped off upon his first venture into the unknown West. John Hawkins's cronies in the Canaries could tell him all that was to be known about "West India "; he took pains to acquire and retain all the information they had to impart. His father's voyages to the western continent, though thirty years old, were fresh in his mind. From the old house in Kinterbury Street his young imagination had sped to the lands beyond the setting of the sun; from the shadow of Teneriffe his man's resolution prompted him thither.

A trader so inspired must know what merchandise to take with him into new markets. What the Spanish Islands in the Gulf of Mexico wanted most, his Canary friends told him, was negroes. After much deliberation he determined to become a slave-trader.

A prodigious quantity of ink and invective has been expended in the denunciation of Hawkins as the pioneer of England's association with the slave-trade. First, as to the fact: he was not the pioneer. John Lok, an Englishman, visiting the West Coast for ivory and gold-dust some ten years earlier, is entitled to the honour. We may therefore cease to execrate Hawkins on that score. Lok's view of the subject was ostensibly that of Las Casas; he saw, in the words of Froude, that "the negroes were people of beastly living, without God, law, religion, or commonwealth, gave some of them opportunity of a life in creation, and carried them off as slaves." Idle as it is to waste words in expressing abomination of the Sixteenth Century Englishman's share in the slave traffic, it is equally futile to pretend that philanthropy was the spring of what he did. Neither Lok nor Hawkins was moved by any altruistic considerations in his action. If, by their removal from their native shores where they were oppressed by their own chiefs, raided by neighbouring tribes, carried off to torture and captivity, and saw their brothers and sisters on the table, and by their transference in slavedom to the Western islands, where they were at least fed instead of being fed on, the negroes were benefited, that was not the reason why Lok captured and sold them to West Indian traders, or Hawkins took shiploads of them to Hispaniola. In a great many cases this was what actually happened. In others, the slavers relieved chiefs of their most troublesome subjects, "who would otherwise have been hanged. Thieves, murderers, and such-like were taken down to the depots and sold."

Yet, when all this has been said, it is on no such pretence that we should hang a defence of the conduct of John Hawkins. Himself would have been startled to find that any such pretence was considered necessary. In his own opinion and the opinion of his time, if he was transgressing any law it was not a law of humanity or morality, but the law of a foreign State — a law quite subject to transgression by a bold man because it was a law of protection and monopoly. Hawkins was merely embarking in a new branch of business, and it was business which was regarded all over the world as perfectly legitimate. Certainly in the England of Elizabeth's day — and we must endeavour to get the perspective of the time if we are to attempt to judge its actions — slave-trading, was regarded with no horror; there was no party in the State to compare with the humanitarian party that properly arises in our own day at the whisper of forced labour; there were very few apostles of the fine gospel of the Brotherhood of Man.

Slavery had horrible results, and to try to depict the attitude of mind in which the Elizabethans approached it is certainly not to set up a defence of the institution. What we are concerned to notice is that John Hawkins contributed no appreciable drop to the volume of misery that resulted from the establishment of negro slavery in America. Every account of him makes Hawkins a man of large heart and generous sympathies. What he did was to divert into his own pockets and those of the people who adventured with him some of the profits that would otherwise have been retained by the Spaniards and the Portugals. Slavery was a very flourishing trade ere ever he touched it. The withering effects of the Spanish occupation upon the natives of the Caribbean Isles had rendered the importation of labour necessary for the planters. Familiar illustrations of the same problem may be found in twentieth century experience, and need no reference here. Charles the Fifth had issued licences for the importation of negroes into the West Indies as long ago as 1515. Sir Clements Markham [2] Has adduced an excellent argument against the reasonableness of blaming John Hawkins for the part of England in the slave trade, by pointing out that whatever obloquy attaches to it must be shared by the whole English people for a period of 250 years: "The English were particularly eager to enter upon the slave-trade; and by the Treaty of Utrecht, in 1713. England at length obtained the *asiento,* giving her the exclusive right to carry on the slave trade between Africa and the Spanish Indies for thirty years. So strong was the party in favour of this trade in England that the contest for its abolition was continued for forty-eight years, from 1759 to 1807."

Just two hundred and thirty years after John Hawkins's first slaving voyage began, there was a debate in the House of Commons in which the very arguments that would have appealed to the Elizabethans were used. I have a report of a speech by Colonel Tarleton, in which he contrasted the lenity of the West India government with the savage ferocity of the African princes in their effects upon the life of a negro. And he added that "if we were inclined to relinquish the traffic, the other nations of Europe would not follow our example, but would make their advantage of our folly. The Dutch and the French would deride us for giving up our share in a beneficial commerce, which would nevertheless go on. The losses would be ours; the profit would be theirs. An equal number of slaves would continue to be imported into the West Indies, and the case of the African would be exactly the same, whether he crossed the Atlantic in an English or any other European bottom." If this contention prevailed upon the British House of Commons for many years against the eloquence of Wilberforce, it is surely foolish to condemn Hawkins for yielding to it more than two centuries before, when the traffic had the blessing of the Church, and he was able to induce his own Queen to join him in it. This is a somewhat inordinate digression from the narrative; but most of the writers on the subject take so hurried and partial a view of it, barely mentioning Hawkins's slaving voyages as a national infamy, that some detailed consideration seemed necessary. It is more conveniently dealt with here than during the description of the voyages.

Having, then, returned to Plymouth from the last of those divers voyages to the Isles of the Canaries before he ventured farther afield, Hawkins had fully made up his mind as to the destination of his next, the "merchandise" he would carry, and the means by which he would do his business. That "diligent inquisition" of his at Santa Cruz had borne its fruit, and he was prepared to risk all that had to be risked in order to establish himself as a trader to the West Indies. Up to the present time, though he was a Protestant, and his brother was encouraging the French Protestant privateers, and John, though much at sea, knew all the lively doings of Plymouth Sound and Cattewater, yet he was friendly with the Spaniards, and did most of his business with them. He did not go about his West Indian adventures of set purpose to come into conflict with the Spanish government; but if a collision did occur he was bound to take the chances of it.

Still, as I have said, the decision at which he had arrived during his voyages to the Canaries was momentous. It was, in fact, the first step towards that irregular warfare between the private squadrons of English adventurers and the Imperial fleets of Spain which terminated in dire catastrophe for King Philip. It is not possible to agree with those writers who suggest that Hawkins was surprised by the issue, and had no expectation that his venture would end in conflict. It is true that the Spanish merchants encouraged him in the idea, and that his cargoes were welcomed in the islands; but none knew better than Hawkins how jealously the Spanish Government guarded all the secrets of their Western possessions, how determined they were that the ships of other nations should not plough the waters of the Gulf of Mexico or trade in their harbours; they had El Dorado, and they meant to keep it to themselves. This determination, this jealousy, were menaced by his first voyage to Hispaniola; the man who projected it could not be ignorant of its possible consequences. Hawkins was a longsighted man; he saw at least as far as that. He was also a dogged man, slow to arrive at a decision, immovable in it when once it was taken.

On his return to Plymouth, he had concluded that the affair was a little bigger than he cared to undertake entirely on his own responsibility. He communicated his idea to certain friends. Four years before, Hawkins had been married to Katherine Gonson, daughter of Benjamin Gonson, Treasurer of the Navy. He thus secured an alliance which was to have an important influence upon his career. The Gonson family had been closely associated with the Navy for many years. William Gonson, father of Hawkins's *beau-père*, had been treasurer in Henry VIII.'s time, when old William Hawkins commanded *The Great Galley*, and Benjamin had married Ursula Hussey, daughter of an Admiralty Judge. In addition to the Gonsons, he had many other influential friends in London.

It was to them that Hawkins turned now for assistance in his venture. Some of them were great merchants, and it is evidence of the high repute in which his capabilities were held that they found it good and lent it countenance and financial support. It was a scheme more daring than any Englishman had ever propounded, but they knew that if any Englishman could carry it through, Hawkins was the man. "The first Englishman," says a contemporary, [3] "that gave any attempt on the coasts of West India was Sir John Hawkins, Knight: who there and in that attempt, as in many others sithens, did and hath proved himself to be a man of excellent capacity, great government, and perfect resolution. For before he attempted the same it was a matter doubtful and reported the extremest limit of danger to sail upon those coasts..." Benjamin Gonson knew all this, and so did Sir Lionel Ducket, Sir Thomas Lodge, Sir William Winter, Mr. Bronfield, and others to whom the plan was unfolded. But they made no difficulty about providing the money and the ships: they all "liked so well of his intention," as Hakluyt puts it, "that they became liberal contributors and adventurers in the action."

The expedition was fitted out at Plymouth. It consisted of three cockleshells, as we should consider them now: the *Solomon*, the flagship, of 120 tons burthen; the *Swallow*, of 100 tons, one Hampton being captain; and the *Jonas*, of 40 tons. Froude has expressed surprise at the dimensions of the ships; he speaks of them as "inconceivably small." But even in our own day, a ketch-rigged vessel not so large as the *Swallow* annually makes two round trips across the stormy Western Ocean from Plymouth. And no doubt Hawkins thought he was respectably equipped. He had under him all told about a hundred men, "for fear of sickness and other inconveniences, whereunto men in long voyages are commonly subject."

In October, 1562, then, the road to the West Indies was inaugurated for the English. The vessels weighed at Plymouth, and shaped a course for the Canaries. At Santa Cruz he was among his old enthusiastic friends. They knew of his project, wished him luck in it, and gave him and Hampton and their men "friendly entertainment." Whereafter they left the islands to embark upon the real business of the cruise. They cast anchor off Sierra Leone, and began to collect negroes and other goods. He "got into his possession, partly by the sw"orde, and partly by other meanes, to the number of 300 negroes at the least, besides other merchandises which that country yieldeth." Hawkins had been to the Guinea Coast before, and knew the trade. He did not give offence by competing with the Government depots for his booty; he picked up slaves where he could get them with the least amount of fuss, and we may be sure that the "sworde" was not employed a great deal. The local chiefs never showed much backwardness about disposing of their prisoners of war and their criminals; it was much more profitable than beheading them and eating them, or feeding them in captivity. The manner of the transaction necessitated a long stay on the coast; but when he had his three hundred blacks safely on board, Hawkins made short work of the rest of it. "He sailed over the ocean sea unto the island of Hispaniola."

So had Columbus sailed over the ocean sea exactly eighty years before, and on the coast of Hispaniola lost and abandoned the *Santa Maria* during the voyage which discovered the New World. In this island, which he named "Espagnola," or Little Spain, there were about two millions of people when the Spaniards took possession of it. They were of a low type, and, according to Spanish authorities, deficient in intellect, morals, and physique. They were effectually exterminated by thirty years of abject slavery imposed upon them by adventurers who were attracted by fabulous stories of the golden wealth of Espagnola. Long before that, the negro traffic had begun, and it was maintained in great volume all through the sixteenth century. The history of Hayti serves in a measure to vindicate the arguments of those who said that their removal to the West Indies was good for the blacks; they could endure labour under conditions which were death to the Caribs, and they thrived upon it, increased and multiplied, took possession of the country and rule it at this day.

Hawkins struck the island on the North, and his flotilla dropped anchor at Port Isabella. His first proceedings were the very pattern of diplomacy. It was true, he said, that he had three hundred negroes with him, and he was willing to sell them if he could obtain permission. But that was not his primary object; he had been driven out of his course while on a voyage of exploration, and he wanted money and supplies. The local Spanish authorities saw nothing wrong in this. There was a state of peace between England and Spain. It was true that they had general orders with regard to the treatment of foreigners who arrived in those waters; but this foreigner was harmless so far as they knew. He had things to sell which the people of Espagnola wanted to buy. Black labour was in great demand, and it would have been rejecting the good gifts of Providence and transgressing the general desire to have allowed this first foreign importer to go away without achieving the projected deal. They therefore made terms with him, advantageous both to them and to him, and chanced what the Government of Madrid would say about it. How that fell out is in the sequel.

At Isabella, Hawkins "had reasonable utterance of his English Commodities, as also of some part of his Negroes," Hakluyt says, "trusting the Spaniards no further than that, by his own strength, he was able to master them." Assuredly, John Hawkins would never make the mistake of trusting strangers beyond reasonable bounds; but there is ample evidence to show that his relations, not only with the planter purchasers of his wares, but also with the authorities, were perfectly amicable. There was no occasion for any display of force. From Isabella, Hawkins moved on to Puerto Plata, and repeated the performance; he finished his bartering at Monte Cristi. The arrangement with the Governor of the island was that he should sell two hundred of his blacks and leave the others with the authorities in case of any difficulty about the duty. He received (still quoting Hakluyt) "in those three places by way of exchange, such a quantity of merchandise, that he did not only lade his own three ships with hides, ginger, sugar, and some quantity of pearls; but he freighted also two other Hulks with hides and other like commodities, which he sent into Spain." The fate of the cargoes thus consigned to King Philip's own dominions is also part of the sequel.

Hawkins had good cause to be pleased with the issue of his first adventure into the West. It had been more successful than there had been any absolute reason to expect. If on his arrival at the Port of Isabella he trusted the Spaniards "no further than that by his own strength he was able to master them," the excellent reception that had awaited him evidently calmed a good many of his suspicions, or he would not have embarked any part of his gains in cargoes for Spain. This was enough for an initial step, and he ventured no farther into the Spanish seas, but stood out into the Atlantic, and steered for England. He arrived in Plymouth in September, 1563, nearly a year after his departure. He was received with much joy by his wife and his brother William. He found his son Richard, now aged three, grown a year bigger and taller; his business prospered, his star was in the ascendant. The townspeople were glad to see the Captain back again. His partners in the enterprise were well pleased with his success. And all the rejoicing and all the congratulations offered to the first Englishman who had opened the route for English trade to the golden west were expressed in complete ignorance of the momentous fact that this exploit had in reality opened another vista — the long vista of conflict and bloodshed in which Spain and England were engaged for thirty years.

The Captain himself was not long without an inkling of the fact. Not many days after his own arrival in Plymouth, there came post-haste his friend Hampton, who had sailed with him in the *Swallow*. Hampton had been despatched by Hawkins with the cargoes of hides to Spain. They were consigned to an Englishman in Cadiz named Tipton, who was to dispose of them to the best advantage in that port, where they were a good marketable commodity. Hampton's story was disappointing in itself, and alarming for the future. He had nothing to show for the cargoes. Immediately upon their arrival, Philip, through the officers of the Inquisition, had seized and confiscated them. It was also given out that an order had been sent to the Governor of Hispaniola to regard the 125 slaves left there with him as forfeit. As for Hampton, he had lost Hawkins's hides and run a considerable risk of his own skin, for he had fled from Spain with the familiars of the Inquisition at his heels.

Indeed, the Inquisition was saving up store of vengeance for a day of reckoning to be appointed by the seamen of Plymouth and the Western ports. This was one more count in the long indictment. Hawkins was enraered: the loss to himself and his fellow-adventurers was 40,000 ducats. It was not to be borne in patience. He set in motion all the machinery on which he could lay his fingers for the coercion of Philip into a more reasonable temper. He wrote to Philip himself; probably he had been in the presence of the Spanish monarch a few years before when the latter landed at Plymouth and was lavishly entertained by the Corporation (of which Hawkins was a member) at a cost of £300. Philip saw accurately in Hawkins the forerunner of the English merchant-adventurers who were to be stout thorns in his side for so many years. It was the beginning of his almost superstitious hatred of the man and his name. He would have no parley with him. No eloquence of argument, no fury of threats would move him. Finding personal appeal of none avail, Hawkins turned to his influential friends in London, and brought the Government and the Court to his aid — with just as little effect. A letter from Queen Elizabeth to King Philip asking consideration for her subject was fruitless. She commanded Sir Thomas Challoner, her Ambassador at Madrid, to intercede for Hawkins, and help him to the utmost of his power. Philip was obdurate, and told Challoner to warn the English that mischief would arise if the visit to the Indies were repeated. Hawkins talked of going to Madrid on the business. Challoner entreated him to stay at home — Challoner's sympathies were with Spain, for which he had fought under Charles V.: he was half a Spaniard.

So the wrangle went on for nearly a year. In July, 1564, Challoner wrote to Hawkins telling him that there was no chance of obtaining any favour from the Spanish Court, and advising him to give four or five thousand ducats to some favourite of King Philip's to ask for the forfeited goods, prescribing that the balance should be handed over to the agents of Hawkins. John Hawkins did nothing of the sort. He sat in Plymouth brooding over his wrongs and meditating his vengeance. The illicit war was now declared. Philip's warning was communicated to the Government, and Sir William Cecil begged the Queen to forbid any more expeditions of the sort. But the Queen at this time had a keener insight than Cecil's into the real issue that was at stake; the next time Hawkins went westward he sailed in a Queen's ship.

[1] Hakluyt.
[2] Introduction to "Hawkins's Voyages."
[3] John Davis: "World's Hydrographical Description."

Chapter V - Second Voyage to the West Indies

Hawkins acted with characteristic caution in the steps he took to place himself even with King Philip. He never hurried a decision; he revolved pros and cons; he exhausted all other methods before he proceeded to the extreme. He had been disputing with Spain over those unhappy cargoes of hides for nearly a year. In July, Challoner's letter informed him of the hopelessness of his case; in October, his second expedition sailed. Hawkins was slow of resolution because of a native deliberation in all his works, not from any weakness of his character, for in action he was the promptest of men. He now had a definite grievance to redress, and Spain should pay for it

Sagacious and wily in counsel as he was ready in deed, Hawkins knew that this had become a bigger affair than could be properly tackled by a private company of adventurers; he made the Queen a partner with him in his enterprise. Elizabeth liked a resolute man, an adventurous man, above all a capable man; such a man she recognised in John Hawkins. Against the advice of Cecil — and these proceedings were much too strong for his stomach — she went into the business to the extent of lending Hawkins her famous ship the *Jesus of Lubek,* a vessel of 700 tons. At little risk and at great profit, she thought, a severe lesson might be administered to Philip. The cold sweat into which he had been thrown by the first descent of Hawkins upon the West Indies showed that in that remote corner of the world was a spot where pinpricks would reach him; Hawkins was an auxiliary arm which would keep Philip busy, and distract his attention from other projects that might be annoying to his sister-in-law.

Nominally, England and Spain were on terms of peace and friendship; in fact, the crisis was gathering; this was a means of staving off a more expensive form of warfare. Englishmen in 1564 could not have failed to read the adumbration of 1588. Again, this was an assertion of a truth which was yearly becoming of more vital consequence to England — the truth that there is no Hen upon the seas. If Englishmen wanted to sail in the Caribbean Sea or the Gulf of Mexico, not all the power of Spain should proscribe them. This is important to be observed; also that England placed upon the Spanish Government the onus of seeing that its own laws were obeyed. Hawkins was trading with Spanish settlers in the islands who were very willing to trade with him; if the trade were to be prohibited, upon the Spanish authorities lay the obligation of enforcing the prohibition. In this view of the matter — it was unquestionably the view taken by Elizabeth and by Hawkins — the confiscation of the hides had been perfectly unjustifiable, and savoured more of piracy than anything that the captain himself had done.

So, in the second expedition, in addition to lending her great ship, the Queen took shares; other adventurers were the Earl of Pembroke, the Earl of Leicester, and all the members of the Council except Cecil, whose distaste for the work persisted. Hawkins was instructed in general terms that no wrong must be done to the King of Spain; the particular application of the word to his measures was left to his own defining. Four ships were fitted out and assembled in Plymouth harbour. They were the *Jesus of Lubek;* the *Solomon,* of 140 tons; the *Tiger,* of 50 tons; and the *Swallow,* of 30 tons.

All being ready, Hawkins took leave of his wife and his little boy, and on October 18th went on board the *Jesus* and set sail for the Canaries. The programme was to be much the same as that of the first voyage, but everything was contrived upon a larger scale. He had more ships and greater carrying capacity, and a hundred fighting men in case of need. It is here that we first meet with Hawkins in the capacity of a military seaman; throughout the adventure he proved himself a born strategist, as well as a rough-and-ready diplomatist and a skilled leader. He had with him John Chester, son of Sir William Chester, Anthony Parkhurst, Thomas Woorley, and William Lacie, among other gentlemen in search of adventure and fortune.

A valuable log of the voyage was written by John Sparke, the younger, who sailed with Hawkins, and was a fellow-townsman; he afterwards became Mayor of Plymouth. This may be read in detail in Hakluyt, and it will be found a very illuminating document, exaggerating nothing and extenuating nothing. It is particularly illustrative of the sentiments of the English world of that day with regard to the slaving trade. Here was Sparke, a thorough Puritan, of a Protestant family, whose tendencies were rather strait-laced than otherwise; and he saw nothing amiss in Hawkins's trafficking. In his view the negroes were taken from Africa for their own good and exported to the Western Islands for the good of the Indians, while Philip was duped for the good of the Protestant cause — a very meritorious concatenation. Sparke does not express these sentiments in these words or anything like them; but they are plain to be read between his vivid lines.

Shortly after leaving Plymouth, Hawkins fell in with the *Minion,* another ship of the Queen's Majesty, and the *John Baptist* of London, bound in company to the Guinea Coast on the slaving business. We shall hear more of them hereafter. They kept company at intervals during the voyage to the Canaries. Tempestuous weather and contrary winds being encountered off Finisterre, Hawkins put into Ferrol on the 25th, and remained there till the 30th, being rejoined in the port by the *Minion,* which had been separated from him in the storm. It was while at Ferrol that Hawkins issued his much-quoted sailing orders to his squadron. They were these (the spelling is modernised): —

"The small ships to be always ahead and aweather of the *Jesus;* and to speak, twice a day, with the Jesus at least.

"If in the day, the ensign to be over the poop of the *Jesus;* or in the night, two lights: then shall all the ships speak with her.

"If there be three lights aboard the *Jesus,* then doth she cast about.

"If the weather be extreme, that the small ships cannot keep company with the *Jesus,* then all to keep company with the *Solomon;* and forthwith to repair to the island of Teneriffe, to the northward of the road of Sirroes.

"If any happen to any misfortune; then to shew two lights and to shoot off a piece of ordnance.

"If any lose company, and come in sight again; to make three yaws and strike the mizzen three times.

"Serve God daily; love one another; preserve your victuals; beware of fire, and keep good company."

There is a ring of Thorough about these sentences. The last is peculiarly fine in expression, and, as was suggested before, makes no bad rule of conduct, taken in its modern significance. "Keep good company," of course, means that the ships were to sail in consort so far as possible.

Without noteworthy adventure they arrived at Teneriffe. At the port of Adecia he went ashore in a pinnace, but found himself the subject of a hostile demonstration by some fourscore men, armed with arquebuses, halberds, pikes, and swords. Apparently, they were unaware of the identity of the expedition. As soon as he saw what the situation was, Hawkins got his boat out of range of the fire-arms, and announced himself, saying that his business was with the Governor, Peter de Ponte. De Ponte was at Santa Cruz, but his son Nicholas was among the officers on shore at Adecia, and at Hawkins's request he ordered the soldiers to retire. The captain then landed and made known the wants of his squadron. The preliminary difficulties over, the old friendly relations were re-established. Hawkins got his fleet victualled, and trimmed the mainmast of the *Jesus,* which had been sprung during the gales. As soon as de Ponte heard that Hawkins was at the island, he journeyed from Santa Cruz to greet him, "and gave him as gentle entertainment as if he had been his own brother." A week thus passed, and on the night of November 15th Hawkins gave his *adios* to de Ponte and the islanders, and set sail for the Guinea Coast and his negro hunting.

There was one incident on the way in which his seamanlike skill and promptitude were displayed. Five days out from Teneriffe, the *Jesus's* pinnace, sailing beside the big ship, with two men on board, was through carelessness capsized. There was a brisk breeze, and the *Jesus* was far away to leeward and the boat out of sight before the ship could be put about. It was Hawkins himself who marked by the sun the spot where the accident had occurred, and he who directed the course of the rescuers in the "great boat," manned by two dozen of the strongest oarsmen in the crew. In the circumstances nobody expected to see the two unhappy wights again, but they were discovered sitting on the keel of the overset boat and brought on board, while the pinnace was recovered. Having saved their lives, Hawkins probably quarter-decked them and rated them soundly for their stupidity: he had a rough tongue for anything like incompetence and folly.

They touched at Cape Blanco and at Cape Verde; and at the latter place took off a shipwrecked Frenchman who had been living for some time with the blacks. Hawkins had thought to obtain a part of his living cargo there, but Cape Verde was drawn blank. It has been mentioned that the *Minion* and the *John Baptist* were bound to the African coast on the same errand as the *Jesus* and her consorts. Leaving Teneriffe before them, the *Minion's* men had fore-stalled them at Cape Verde, and they found the birds too wild. Leaving on December 7th, they made for Jeba, stopping by the way at Alcantraz Island, a place inhabited only by sea-birds. The two big ships rode at anchor here while the *Tiger* and the *Swallow* were sent to an adjoining island, La Formio, where eighty men of arms were landed and pursued a number of negroes of the tribe named by them Sapies. The blacks showed fight, and being unac-quainted with the effect of firearms, showed no alarm at the discharge of the arquebuses till one of their number received a shot in his thigh. There were no signs of large settlements, and Hawkins, seeing that he could not hope to get any number of slaves there, left. He also abandoned the intention of going into Jeba, because he found so many shoals on the coast and was afraid of getting his two big ships stuck aground.

The first haul of negro flesh and blood was therefore made on the island of Sambula. Here they found orderly villages and well-tilled lands, but the na-tive Sapies in a state of subjection to a cannibal tribe which Sparke names the "Samboses" — the original "Samboes." The latter fled at the white men's ap-proach, and Hawkins conducted as many as he could get of the former from one condition of slavery to another. The boats were filled with rice, fruit, and "mill," and they departed on December 21st, having lost one man — a greedy fellow who wanted an extra share of "pompions," which he had found good eating, went unarmed to raid them, and had his throat cut by some natives in ambush among the trees.

On the succeeding day Hawkins conducted an expedition in person up a river "called Callowsa." This was effected by means of boating parties, the two big ships being left at anchor in the estuary, while the two smaller went up some distance to serve as a base for the boats. The result of three days' operations was "two caravels laden with negroes."

Then came the assault upon the town of Bymba, the one misadventure of the expedition. The Portuguese factors on the coast had told Hawkins that the place would be an easy and a profitable capture. They narrated glowing stories of the gold it contained, and of the slaves that might be impressed, and of the weakness of its defences. Forty men in armour and arms were landed by boat, the Portuguese acting as guides. The tall tales of the treasure of Bymba demoralised all Hawkins's plans, for they induced his men to split into very small companies and thus to go raiding houses in search of gold. They were overwhelmed by the savages, who chased them down to their boats, and shot arrows at them as they scrambled through the shoal water or attempted to swim for their lives. Hawkins, at the head of a dozen men, had gone right through the village in good order in search of slaves, and now returning found all the rest of his party routed, a couple of hundred yelling natives on the shore, and the boats' crews in pretty plight, many of them wounded, drowning, or suffocated in the mud. He gave fight and forced his wav to the boats, and so got clear of the pestilential place. The casualties among the English were seven killed, including Field, captain of the *Solomon,* and twenty-seven wounded. All they got for their pains was the addition of ten negroes to their tale of slaves. Here is Sparke's picture of Hawkins in the moment of adversity: —

"The Captain, in a singular wise manner, carried himself, with countenance very cheerful outwardly, as though he did little weigh the death of his men, nor yet the hurt of the rest (although his heart was inwardly broken in pieces for it): done to this end, that the Portuguese being with him, should not presume to resist against him, nor take occasion to put him to further displeasure or hindrance for the death of our men."

Cool, calculating, apparently dispassionate as ever, Hawkins was deeply grieved by the punishment of his comrades; but he allowed nothing to interfere with his aims, and he was as wary after a bad buffet in a savage country as he was in a counting-house deal at home in Plymouth.

They left, on December 30th, for Taggarin, and on New Year's Day of 1565 the two small ships and the boats parted company with the *Jesus* and the *Solomon,* and went negro-hunting up the river Casseroes. They were away five days, "trafficking," and must have made a large number of captures and purchases, for, with just one further trip by the *Swallow* alone, the business on the Guinea Coast was completed. The climate of Sierra Leone was deadly to white men, or Hawkins would have taken greater store of slaves to the West Indies this second voyage. The Portuguese had informed him of a forthcoming battle between the tribes of Sierra Leone and Taggarin, and he would have waited for it, following the now usual course of purchasing from the victor his prisoners of war at a cheap rate, but for the deaths and sickness which were reducing his men, "which came by the contagiousness of the place, which made us to make hast away."

Haste they did, at the best pace the flotilla could achieve, westward to the Indies, setting sail on the night of January 18th. They just escaped an ambush prepared for them by the King of Sierra Leone, who missed his chance of seeing "what kind of people we were" by delaying the arrival of his army for a single day. If it had appeared at night when the men of the expedition were all busy filling water in preparation for the voyage across the Atlantic, there might have been another story to write. But, as the chronicler of this piratical, slave-raiding, buccaneering company said with all sincerity, "God, who worketh all things for the best, would not have it so, and by Him we escaped without danger. His name be praysed for it."

"Almightie God, who never suffereth His elect to perish!"...So Sparke exclaims a little later, in describing the terrible twenty-eight days during which the four ships, with their great company of sailors, soldiers, and slaves, were becalmed in the Atlantic. Quaint evidence of the perfect faith they had in the morality and righteousness of their business, horrible as its details are. The calm was only varied by brief fierce storms of contrary wind till February 16th, when "Almightie God...sent us the ordinary brise, which is the North-west winde, which never left us till wee came to an Island of the Canybals, called Dominica."

It was on March 9th that Hawkins made signal to his little fleet to heave-to off the Dominican coast, and from that time till May 31st he was busily engaged upon his mission of getting even with King Philip for the trick played upon him at the end of his first voyage. He knew that the task he had taken in hand was both difficult and dangerous; but he had omitted no necessary thing by way of preparation for all possible emergencies. He was prepared with his story to explain his presence in those waters. He was prepared with goods to sell which the Spaniards wanted to buy. If any official punctilios stood in the way of his trade, he was prepared with ample force to back up what he conceived to be his right to trade. Above all he was prepared with his own inimitable *sang-froid* and adroitness. John Hawkins's nerve never deserted him. He could always preserve his British stolidity, whatever the situation, however delicate, however perilous; and his subordinate officers and his men had perfect faith in his ability to deal with every problem that arose, and to get them out of every hole into which they tumbled. He set forthwith about the business of disposing of the 400 negroes he had with him, and never relaxed his effort till they were all on shore and paid for in various parts of the West Indies.

The great trouble of the prolonged voyage across the Atlantic had been shortness of water, and Hawkins only delayed long enough at inhospitable Dominica to obtain water for the slaves. They lay off shore one night, and the next day set sail to the south-east. The principal settlement and the biggest market at that time in the West Indies was Hispaniola; but to have gone there after what happened in 1562 would have been to put his head into the lion's mouth. Hawkins hoped to circumvent King Philip by going to the more remote parts of his Western possessions and dealing with men who might know less of him in places where his armada would be more formidable than in the great island of Santo Domingo. Therefore he made for the Spanish Main — the northern mainland of the South American continent, the shores of what is now Venezuela. He touched first at the island of Margarita, where he found the few Spanish settlers very willing to entertain him hospitably enough and victual his ships, but unwilling to hear of trading with him. The Governor of the island was decidedly hostile, and set about harassing Hawkins by every measure he could devise. Not only did he forbid a pilot whom Hawkins had engaged to go with him along the coast, but he took steps to acquaint greater authorities than himself with the fact that the dreadful "Achines" was on the coast. He sent a caravel express across the Caribbean Sea to Santo Domingo to inform the Viceroy of the Spanish Indies. The Viceroy had already warned the settlers on the Main against trafficking with any foreigners who might attempt to violate the Spanish monopoly. He now re-doubled the emphasis of the prohibition.

But this is anticipating events. Margarita was drawn blank. The Governor was able to put a check on any desire that the settlers might have enter-tained to trade with Hawkins. But the Englishman's display of force had an ominous look; there was no doubt that with the ships and men at his disposal he might have imposed his will on Margarita and anticipated some of the lat-er exploits of his kinsman Drake. The Governor evidently feared that where complaisance failed him Hawkins might try coercion; and he therefore com-manded the withdrawal of all the inhabitants from the town, and assembled them on the hills behind, where the adventurers could have them at no ad-vantage, if indeed force were to be used. The captain, however, had no idea of using force in such a case. He saw that in any event there would be little chance of profitable trade in the island, and he wanted to get on with his work before the narrow seas became too hot to hold him. He went his way. He slipped across to the Main, and two days' sailing brought him to Cumana.

Hawkins himself went ashore in his pinnace to sound the settlers as to the prospects of business. They appeared to be soldiers newly arrived in that region, and declared that they could not raise enough capital among them to invest in a single negro. They were, however, able to show him a convenient place for watering his ships, at Santa Fé, a couple of leagues away, where the "Indians" came down to the shore and traded with the newcomers, bringing cakes made of maize — a novelty to their eyes — poultry, potatoes, also new, "the most delicate roots that may be eaten, and do far exceed our parsnips or carrots," and pines. Beads, pewter whistles, glasses, and knives were the arti-cles bartered for these welcome provisions. They departed from Cumana on March 28th, and coasted eastward for three days, keeping well inshore. Hawkins himself generally sailed in his pinnace close to the land to spy it out. "Burboroata" was the next place at which they called. It was probably at La Guayra, or near it. Hawkins anchored his ships off the town and went on shore to speak with the authorities. The colloquy was a long and interesting one.

Chapter VI - On the Spanish Main

IN the story of Hawkins's dealings with the Spaniards on the Main, there is much that may seem unmoral and impossible of approval. To modern sense, the way m which he contrived to get rid of his blacks and compensate himself for the misadventure of the previous voyage is thoroughly objection-able. This is no attempt to canonise Hawkins, but some circumstances must be constantly kept in mmd. First, the age had no humanitarian ideas about slave-trading. Next, the English were determined to maintain the franchise of the seas and the right to trade. They did not contest the right of sovereigns to levy import duties on goods landed in their dominions by foreign ships; but they did contest the right of sovereigns to close whole seas to trade. Again, the lively sense of injustice and injury under which Hawkins was suffering must be remembered.

He insisted on trading. He would trade as a plain Englishman who had commodities for sale to any who wanted to buy. He would on his part provide excuses for his appearance m their ports if excuses were required, and reasons why he must require them to purchase his cargoes in order that he might replenish his exchequer and his storeroom — reasons which they could pass on for him to any authority that might manifest an inconvenient tendency to ask questions. Or he would land men and guns and threaten dire things if they still refused. But he would trade. He knew that at the back of him— behind the guns of the *Jesus of Lubek* and the soldiers she carried — was the power of England. He had declared a private war against King Philip; but in that private war he had the sympathy and covert assistance of Queen Elizabeth.

The Spaniards found Hawkins the most troublesome, most persistent Englishman that had ever crossed their path. He was a man of slow speech, but not to be denied. He was a man of slow anger, but terrible in his wrath — the more terrible because its manifestations were so calculated and orderly.

The *pourparlers* with the residents at Burboroata, and with the Governor whom they brought from a distance to their assistance in the matter, provide a fair example of his methods, and of the way in which he proceeded from fair words to force, and finally carried his point. Going ashore to them on his arrival, he bluntly declared that he was an Englishman who had come there to do business. He had some four hundred negroes to sell, and he required a licence to trade. They replied that they were forbidden by the King to traffic with any foreign nation, on penalty of forfeiting their goods, and they requested that he should not molest them further, but "depart as he came; for other comfort he might not look at their hands, because they were subjects, and might not go beyond the law."

Imagine John Hawkins's look-out to the bay where the *Jesus of Lubek* and her consorts lay at anchor. They had sailed from Plymouth exactly seven months before; they had experienced many adventures and endured much hardship; as yet they had done practically no business. And these Spaniards, who wanted his goods, talked to him of laws! See his brows contract a little, and his lips tighten under his beard, as he witnesses the failure of his first overture, and prepares to open the second

They talked of law; he answered that necessity knoweth no law; his necessity was to trade. "For being in one of the Queen of England's *Armados,* and having many soldiers in them, he had need of some refreshing for them, and of victuals, and of money also: without which he could not depart." [1] He told them that he had no ulterior motives; he wanted to trade, not to get them into trouble with their rulers. And why should any trouble be anticipated? He was sailing under the flag of England, and was content to be open and aboveboard; he would do nothing to dishonour his sovereign and his own reputation. What he asked them to do was to supply for themselves an admitted want, in a transaction which would redound to their profit as well as his own. As for the prohibition, it must surely be a mistake so far as he was concerned, and they might deal with him without danger, "because their Princes were in amity one with another, and for our parts we had free traffic in Spain and Flanders" — Philip's own dominions — "and therefore he knew no reason why he should not have the like in all his dominions."

This was clever rather than ingenuous. Hawkins knew full well that the Spaniards wanted the blacks and would be eager to buy if they thought they could do so without risk to themselves; but he knew of the embargo that had been placed against him, and knew that they knew it. They declined to listen to the voice of the tempter; at least they would have nothing to do with him on their own responsibility. They invited him to bring his ships from the bay into the harbour and wait for ten days while they communicated with the Governor of the Province, who resided at sixty leagues' distance. To bring the business to this point had taken four days. Hawkins fetched his ships inside and re-victualed. But he had no intention of waiting ten days there, with his slaves and his men eating their heads off in idleness, on the off-chance of an answer from the Governor which might be favourable or mifavourable. He therefore asked for permission to sell at once "certain lean and sick negroes, which he had in his ships likely to die upon his hands if they were kept ten days," whereas they would be recovered and found fit for work speedily enough if they could be brought on shore. This request, he said further, he was forced to make because without the value of the slaves he could not pay for his provisions.

The officers and the townsmen consulted upon this proposal. They were all itching to do the business if by any means they might get to windward of the authorities. They decided to accept. There was some delay in the consummation of the bargain; the Spaniards naturally wanted to beat down the price, and imagined that the longer they kept Hawkins about, the lower would be the figure at which he would finally sell. They never misjudged a man more completely. At once he took the high hand, and threatened to cast the dust of Burboroata off his feet, taking his blacks with him. This did not suit their book. They were at deadly enmity with the Caribs of the district, they were short of labour, and Hawkins's blacks were much too precious to be allowed to depart. A few were bought immediately. The haggling went on again, and was continued till April 14th, when the Governor appeared upon the scene.

To him, Hawkins made formal petition. He declared that "he was come thither in a ship of the Queen's Majesty of England, being bound to Guinea; and thither driven by wind and weather; so that being come thither, he had need of sundry necessaries for the reparation of the said Navy, and also great need of money for the payment of his soldiers, unto whom he had promised payment; and therefore, although he would, yet they would not depart without it. And for that purpose, he requested licence for the sale of certain of his Negroes; declaring that though they were forbidden to traffic with strangers: yet for that there was great amity between their Princes, and that the thing pertained to our Queen's Highness; he thought he might do their Prince a great service, and that it would be well taken at his hands, to do it in this cause."

It was a glaring false pretence, fully understood on both sides, designed merely to give the Spanish authorities an excuse for presentation to their own conscience and to their superiors. Hawkins got his way. Sitting in Council, the Governor heard the petition and granted the licence. There was another dispute about the King's custom. The duty was 30 ducats on each slave— £8 5s. of the money of that day, and nearer £70 value of our own. Hawkins saw that the buyers at Burboroata were not going to approach the price he wanted for the slaves, and that, if he had to pay this heavy duty, his own profits would be a vanishing quantity. Time was slipping on. He had now exhausted every device but one: he had recourse to that.

"He prepared 100 men, well-armed with bows, arrows, harquebuses, and pikes; with the which he marched to the townards." This was his first armed measure against the Spaniards. The show of hostility set up a panic. The Governor sent him a messenger, "straight, with all expedition," to ask him to state his demands, and to march no further until he had received the answer. Hawkins said the duty must be reduced to 7½ per cent., which was the ordinary custom for wares imported into the West Indies, and not a stiver more would he pay. Further, if they refused to make the abatement, "he would displease them."

It was enough. They had no great wish to be "displeased" after the manner which they knew Hawkins might be expected to adopt, and the Governor sent him word that "all things should be to his content." Hostages were demanded for the performance of the Spaniards' promises, and sent. The traffic in slaves commenced. The poorer settlers having bought all they could afford, the richer sort came down to haggle further about the price. Once more Hawkins had to threaten that he would take his goods elsewhere; once more the threat was successful. By May 4th they had exhausted the market and had done very well indeed in it.

While they were at Burboroata they received further news of the *Minion*, of which we last heard on the Guinea coast. A French captain, Bontemps, of *The Green Dragon*, of Havre, arrived in the harbour telling a moving story of hot encounter with the Portuguese on that coast, of being driven off with only half a cargo of blacks. He was able to inform them that the *Minion* had been in a like strait. Her captain, David Carlet, a supercargo, and a number of seamen had been betrayed by the negroes and captured by the Portuguese — "which was most sorrowful for us to understand."

In some sort, the people at Burboroata had reason to be thankful to Hawkins for his threats of force. He had so effectually awakened their defences that they were fortuitously ready for a sudden attack made by the Caribs on the town on the night of May 3rd, and were able to beat off the enemy with loss. On his departure, the Captain made for Curasao, and traded most profitably for hides, the principal product of the island. Since the occupation of Curagao by the Spaniards forty years before, the cattle introduced from Europe had thriven and increased so remarkably that the beasts were now killed merely for their skins. The tongue of an ox was cut out, and the rest of the carcase left to the birds. In nine days Hawkins had invested to good advantage in hides the money obtained for his negroes at Burboroata, and left. He coasted eastwards along the Main again, sailing inshore in the pinnace himself as of old, rounded Cape de la Vela, and on May 19th arrived at Rio de la Hacha.

By this time the caravel despatched from Margarita had arrived at Santo Domingo, the Viceroy had raged furiously when he learnt that "Achines" was upon his coasts, and had sent an express commission to La Hacha, La Vela, and other places, forbidding the King's subjects to have any dealings with the English marauder. Hawkins learnt this the first day he went on shore to "have talk with the King's Treasurer of the Indies, resident there." But he had foreseen the circumstance, and divined the course of events that would follow. He was not to be disturbed either by the prohibitions or by the threats of the Spaniards. He had some negroes left; the settlers wanted to buy them. Viceroy and Council notwithstanding, he meant to conclude his trading at Rio de la Hacha. The Treasurer told him that they durst not traffic with him, for, if they did, "they should lose all that they did traffick for, besides their bodies, at the magistrate's commandment."

Hawkins smiled at their fears, knew how much they counted for, and quietly advanced the old story. "He was in an Armado of the Queen's Majesty of England," and on the affairs of the Queen. He had been driven out of his course by contrary winds, and he had hoped in these parts to find the same friendly relations existing between honest traders of England and Spain as in Spain itself. There was no reason that he knew of why this should not be so, for perfect amity reigned between King Philip and Queen Elizabeth. Thus he preferred his request to be allowed to trade; if it were not granted, he would see whether he could not argue more forcibly, employing falcons, arquebuses, bows, and pikes, instead of words. He "willed them to determine either to give him licence to trade, or else stand to their own arms!" Experience had taught Hawkins that a lot of argument was nothing but waste of time. The Spaniards wanted his slaves, and the cause of their apparent reluctance to buy was not any fears of the thunders of the Viceroy or the distant displeasure of the Monarch; they believed that by making it as difficult as possible for him to sell they would get a reduction in price corresponding to the size of the obstacles they placed in his way. But they could not carry out this programme twice with Hawkins. Upon the first sign of prevarication he threatened to retaliate with cannon-balls.

The result demonstrated his prescience and the perspicacity of his judgment. At the first suggestion of force, the opposition collapsed partly: they would give him licence to trade if he would reduce the price of his slaves by half. "If it liked him not," they said, "he might do what he would, for they were determined not to deal otherwise with him." There was a saturnine humour in Hawkins's response to this piece of bluff. "You deal too rigorously with me," said he, in effect, to go about to cut my throat in the price of my commodities, which are so reasonably priced that you cannot get them as cheap from any other trader. But, seeing that you've sent me this for supper, Senor Treasurer — I'll see what I can bring you for breakfast." [2]

There was some stir the next morning on board the *Jesus of Lubek,* lying off the town. The men had been entertaining themselves during the parley by watching the crocodiles about the ship. They saw many, "of sundry big-nesses," travelling so far seaward because the volume of river water was so great that "the salt water was made fresh." One of their negroes, filling water, was carried off. But this morning, instead of watching the amphibians and speculating on the origin of the phrase *lachrymae crocodili* (as Sparke does very entertainingly), they had bigger business to do. It was May 21st. Soon after sunrise there was a puff of white smoke from the side of the flagship, and the hoarse voice of a whole-culverin awakened the town of Rio de la Ha-cha. Hawkins had a firm belief in the value of a demonstration of energy. He did not want a sanguinary encounter with the Spaniards; the best way to car-ry his point without it was, he thought, to advertise a bloodthirsty intention as loudly as possible. He got ready his hundred men in armour, and presently a little flotilla of boats left for the shore. Hawkins led in the great boat, with two brass falcons in her bows. The other boats were armed with double-bases.

The King's Treasurer of the Indies and his people did not mean to fight; but for the honour of their boasts and for the sake of appearances they made a good show of opposition. The Treasurer collected 150 footmen and 30 horsemen, with drums and colours, and marched towards the landing place — it was a sandy beach — with every possible demonstration of defiance. They shouted war at the oncoming boats, and waved their flags and their weapons in invitation to the Englishmen to mortal combat. Hawkins knew how to dissipate their martial ardour. At a word from him the gunners trained the two brass falcons on them and fired. They afterwards declared their astonishment at the presence of pieces so large in a boat. The immedi-ate effect of the fire was, Sparke says, that "at every shot they fell flat to the ground; and as we approached near unto them, they broke their array, and dispersed themselves so much for fear of the ordnance, that at last they all went away without their ensign." The horsemen, finely caparisoned, with white leather shields and javelins, made a brave display, and caracoled up and down the sands until the boats' noses grounded — when they also re-tired, and the landing was accomplished.

Hawkins went quietly on with his plans, knowing full surely that he had only to persevere with the attack in order to secure all he wanted, and that any show of pusillanimity would be fatal. He drew up his force on the beach, and marched towards the town. The expected result followed immediately in the shape of a messenger with a flag of truce. "The Treasurer marveiled," said the messenger, "what he meant to do, to come ashore in that order, seeing they had granted every reasonable demand he had made." Hawkins took no notice. This was not to the point, and he marched forward. The messenger then begged him to halt his men and come forward alone to speak with the Treasurer. This Hawkins agreed to do.

Midway between the two forces the parley was held. Hawkins clad in armour, went without any weapon, and of course on foot. The Spanish officer was armed cap-apie, and on horseback. Thus they "communed together." It issued thus — that all Hawkins's requests were conceded, and we hear nothing more about half-price for his goods. Gages were obtained for the performance of the promises made by the Spaniards. Then everything was peaceful for several days. Hawkins had got rid of all his negroes, and was trying to induce the Treasurer to pay a debt left by the Governor of Burboroata upon some of the slaves purchased there. Negotiations on this point were proceeding when the whisper of treachery rose. A captain and a file of soldiers arrived at Rio de la Hacha from some neighbouring place. Hawkins suspected an unfriendly act, immediately broke off all business, and went aboard his ships. When he came ashore again next morning, it was in force, falcons in his boats, and men fully armed. Once more his demonstration of an intention to stand no trifling was fully effective, and he and the Treasurer parted good friends. The Treasurer gave Hawkins a testimonial in writing of his good behaviour while at the port, and Hawkins saluted the Treasurer with a salvo from the bases in his boat.

It would be useless to attempt to decide whether the Spaniards meant treachery or were merely making preparations to withstand any further demands that Hawkins might impose upon them. All that is certain is that they reinforced their strength and got fresh guns. As the ships weighed, the English were surprised to hear the hoarse voices of four falcons set speaking from the town in token of farewell. However, it all ended amicably: Hawkins had done his business, he had got even with King Philip, and he left the Spanish Main on May 31st.

[1] Sparke's Narrative.
[2] *See* Sparke's account of the negotiations.

Chapter VII - The Return to England

By dint of persistence and resource, backed by threats and the determination to carry them into practice if he could not carry his point without them, Hawkins had now finished with his good friend the King's Treasurer of the Indies for the time being. He was to meet him again three years later.

On the last day of May, 1565, then, the *Jesus of Lubek,* the *Solomon,* the *Tiger,* and the *Swallow* hove anchor out of the river mouth, and the flagship led the way to the north. So far as trading in blacks was concerned, the business was over; Hawkins had sold all his slaves. His mercantile instinct was to invest on the spot the money he had obtained in some product of which the value appreciated in Europe; he wanted to go to Jamaica to trade in hides, and set his course for Hispaniola (Santo Domingo). His intention was not to beard in his den the Viceroy whom he had flouted, but simply to feel his way westward through unaccustomed seas to the island of Jamaica.

This purpose was defeated by the prevailing lack of information as to the set of the currents. How jealously the Spaniards guarded all knowledge of the navigation of the Caribbean Sea and the Gulf of Mexico in their effort to preserve El Dorado to themselves has already been stated. As a matter of fact, owing to the westerly stream, Hawkins, fancying that he approached Hispaniola on the South, struck the middle of the Jamaican coast instead, and did not discover his mistake till it was too late to amend. The error was encouraged by a Spaniard of Jamaica whom he had on board, having rescued him from the negroes on the Guinea coast. This gentleman pretended that he knew every land-mark thereabout, and most effectually fogged and befooled the captain. Done in all innocence and good part, it was none the less annoying. Hawkins got so far down to leeward that he could not get up again without a prodigious waste of time, and he abandoned the idea, bemoaning what he considered the loss of a good two thousand pounds' worth of profit if he had been able to call at a Jamaican port.

Resigning himself to a compulsory sacrifice, he coasted the southern shore of Cuba, and unfortunately also overshot the port of Santa Cruz, where he had reckoned that he might be able to make good the loss of the Jamaican deal. He watered at the Isle of Pines, doubled Cape San Antonio, the extreme western point of Cuba, and tacked about between its northern coast and the Florida Keys, intending to go into Havana. Once more he was misled as to its position — this time by a Frenchman. His chronicler Sparke has some contemptuous things to say of these "praters."

All this time Hawkins was doing a good deal of valuable work, taking soundings and noting the currents. On July 8th, a fair westerly wind sprang up, and he decided to wait about no longer, but to take advantage of the breeze and to commence the long voyage to Europe. They doubled Florida Reefs on July 12th, and so got out into the Atlantic again. Since they had struck the Leeward Islands at Dominica on March 9th, they had sailed along the Spanish Main, across the Caribbean Sea, through the Yucatan Straits, into the Gulf of Mexico and out again, traversing many seas that English sailors had never seen before. They marvelled greatly at the extraordinary strength of the currents prevailing in these waters. Owing to this phenomenon of the Gulf of Mexico, they lost two boats on the very day they rounded Florida Cape — the pinnace of the *Jesus* and the *Solomon's* boat, which had been sent to one of the islands to find water. They expected never to pick them up again, and had resigned their companies to the tender mercies of the cannibals of the coast, unless they should haply find their way 400 miles north to the River of May, where there was a French station. On November 14th they were recovered after the ships had beat about several days on the off-chance of seeing them, the *Jesus* bearing a light in her topgallant by night to assist the eager eyes of the lost mariners on that lonely sea.

Hawkins coasted the Atlantic shore of Florida for 120 leagues. He resumed his old practice of sailing inshore himself in the pinnace. The great want of the flotilla was water. He had heard of the French colony established on the coast at the mouth of the May River, and, believing that wherever the Frenchmen were he would be able to find opportunity of watering and revictualing his ships, he never left searching for them, and sailed the pinnace into every creek till he succeeded. He had been told that they were to be discovered in about 28° N. lat., but found the river rather more than two degrees further north. Entering the estuary he saw a French ship of about 80 tons and a couple of pinnaces, whose officers informed him of a fort two leagues further up the stream, held by their captain, one M. Laudonniere, and a number of soldiers. Hawkins took one of his small ships up, and had a far more hearty welcome than he expected. Indeed, Laudonniere was much more rejoiced to see Hawkins than he to see the Frenchman, keenly as he was in want of water and provisions. He was entertained with such hospitaHty as the colonists could provide, and harrowed with a sorry story of misery and suffering. Whatever might be done in later years by the French in other parts of the world, it was clear that they were no fit colonisers for Florida.

Laudonnière and his men had been on the River of May fourteen months, since May of 1564; on their arrival they were about 200 all told. They had taken with them little provision, and did not seem to have the energy or the intelligence to get a living for themselves out of what was certainly a rich country. As Sparke observed, "they were soldiers who expected to live by the sweat of other men's brows." They ate up all the maize they could buy from the natives, and then, in order to get rations of millet, they consented to serve in military capacity a local chief against his enemies. Finally, they were reduced to eating acorns. This, notwithstanding the fact that the river was full of fish, to be had for the catching, and the soil fruitful of grapes, corn, and roots. The English heard the story with amazement which something diluted their sympathy. Eighty of the Frenchmen had revolted some time before, clapped Laudonnière in prison, and run off with one of the ships and a pinnace to go buccaneering in the West Indies. They had a high piratical time, looting Spanish ships and settlements, till twenty of them were captured by the Spaniards and strung up by the neck. The other sixty returned to Florida — to be served in like manner by their incensed comrades. The survivors had, in the interim, been at war with the Floridans, and their numbers were sorely reduced. The few remaining when Hawkins arrived had about ten days' provisions in sight.

"In which perplexity, our captain seeing them, spared them out of his ship twenty barrels of meal, and four pipes of beans; with divers other victuals and necessaries which he might conveniently spare; and to help them the better homewards, whither they were bound before our coming, at their request we spared them one of our barks of 50 tons." [1]

Hawkins had first offered to transport the whole colony to France; but Laudonnière did not accept this proposal. He was afraid that Hawkins "would attempt something in Florida in the name of his mistresse." Such was the reputation of "Achines de Plimua." The Englishman was therefore contented to sell Laudonniere one of his smaller ships for 700 crowns, and let him have provisions and shoes for his barefooted company. The Frenchman was duly grateful for this opportune relief, and in an account of his life (Paris, 1586) he set forth, under the heading of "The Arrival and Courtesy of M. Hawkins to the Distressed Frenchmen in Florida," that the English seaman "gave divers presents to the principal officers of my company according to their qualities: so that I may say we received as many courtesies of the General as it was possible to receive of any man living. Wherein, doubtless, he hath won the reputation of a good and charitable man, deserving to be esteemed as much of us all as if he had saved all our lives."

Sparke gives a quaint narrative of the observations made by Hawkins and his officers in Florida. To this voyage, possibly, we may attribute the introduction of tobacco into England. The Frenchmen at the River of May had been staving off the pangs of hunger by smoking the seductive weed. Sparke says:

"The Floridans when they travel have a kind of herb dried, who with a cane and a earthen cup in the end, with fire, and the dried herbs put together, do suck through the cane the smoke thereof; which smoke satisfieth their hunger, and therewith they live four or five days without meat and drink. And this all the Frenchmen used for this purpose; yet do they hold opinion withal, that it causeth water and phlegm to void from their stomachs."

Another visible result of this voyage is the name of Hawkins County on the map of Tennessee.

The three ships now remaining left the River of May on the 28th of July. Contrary winds forced them to go northwards still, and their provisions ran very low. Sparke piously remarks that they would have despaired of ever coming home again, "had not God, of His goodness, better provided for us than our deserving." This was by setting them on the Bank of Newfoundland, where they arrived on St. Bartholomew's Eve, 23rd of August. Cod was then obtained in some quantity, the ships being becalmed for a day, and more was purchased from a couple of French ships encountered on the 29th. The methods of adventurers in those latitudes were evidently not in very good odour with French mariners, for we are naively informed of their surprise at getting anything at all in payment for their fish!

Then, "with a good large wind," they crossed the Atlantic without further adventure or mishap, and arrived at Padstow, on the North Coast of Cornwall, on the 20th of September: "with a loss of twenty persons in all the voyage, as with great profit to the venturers of the said voyage, so also to the whole realm, in bringing home both gold, silver, pearls, and other jewels in great store."

The "great profit" amounted to about 60 per cent, for which the adventurers were inclined to be very thankful.

Hawkins, having brought his three ships into the little harbour of Padstow, immediately wrote to Queen Elizabeth informing her that he had made a most fortunate voyage, and then hurried across Cornwall to Plymouth and home. There was a brief stay with Dame Katherine and his little son Richard, and a consultation with his brother. He was soon on his way to London. He must have known that the voyage would greatly increase his popularity in the country and the esteem in which he was held at Court; but the bluff seaman was hardly prepared for the reception that awaited him. In the words of Froude, he was the hero of the hour, "affecting the most unconscious frankness, and unable to conceive that he had done anything at which the King of Spain could take offence." He told the Queen: "I have always been a help to all Spaniards and Portugal that have come in my way, without any form or prejudice offered by me to any of them, although many times in this tract they have been in my power." An interesting document may be found in the State papers, a letter signed by some of the adventurers, relating to the *Jesus,* which lay at Padstow at the time:

"Whereas the Quene's Matie did of late at the petition and desier of the right honorable the Erie of Pembrock and the Erie of Leyceter graunte vnto their honors her Ma'ie's shipp called the *Jesus* with ordinance tackle and apparell, beinge in sort able and meete to serve a voyage to the Costes of Aflfrica and America, which shipp with her ordinance tackle and apparell was praysed by ffoure indifferent persons to be worth ijm xijli xvs. ijd., for the answeringe whereof to the Quene's Ma'ie the said Erles did become bounde to her Highnes either to redeliver the said shipp the *Jesus* at Gillingham before the feast of Christmas next comynge with her ordnance tackle and apparell in as good and ample manner as the same was at the tyme of the recevinge, or els to paie unto her Highnes the foresaid ijm xijli xvs. ijd. at that daie. And now forasmuche as we do understand that the said shipp the *Jesus* is returned into this realme in savetie from the viadge aforesaid pretended, and presently remayneth in the west countrie in a harborowgh called Padstowe, from whence she cannot be convenyently brought abowt to Gillingham before the springe of the next yere, and that the said Lordes are contented to allowe unto her Matie as well for the wearing of the said shipp her ordinance tackle and apparell, as also for the chardges which maye be sustayned for the bringinge abowt of the said shipp to the harborowgh of Gillingham, the some of Veli readie monney to be paid into her Highnes office of the Admyraltie to Beyamyn Gonson her graces Treasurer, which some of Veli we her Highnes officers whose names are underwritten do thinke the same sufficyent for the repayringe and furnyshinge of the ordinance tackle and apparell with the said shipp in as ample manner as the same was delivered to the said Erles.

"Written the xxiijth of October 1565."

The document was signed by Gonson and the Wynters, and by William Holstock. Apparently the £500 compensation was accepted, for we find the *Jesus* granted to Hawkins again next year.

The story of the voyage became general currency, and one of its incidents — the crocodiles at Rio de la Hacha — is thought to have inspired Shakespeare's lines in "Henry VI.":

> "As the mournful crocodile
> With sorrow snares relenting passengers."

He was received by the Queen, and dined at the Palace, where he met De Silva, the Spanish Ambassador. Hawkins maintained his show of *naiveté*. He kept up the same character that he had assumed before the Spanish officials in the West Indies — except that he neither threatened the Ambassador nor fired off brass cannon at him. He told him where he had been, and what business he had done, and gave him a full account of the expedition, albeit he did not mention the little display of force and expenditure of gunpowder at Burboroata and Rio de la Hacha. Hawkins had washed the smell of saltpetre off his hands long ago; and what did it matter in any case, since no bones were broken on either side?

De Silva wrote an account of the affair to King Philip; this was in November. "I met him in the Palace," said he, "and invited him to dine with me. He gave me a full account of his voyage, keeping back only the way in which he had contrived to trade at our ports. He assured me, on the contrary, that he had given the greatest satisfaction to all the Spaniards with whom he had had dealings, and had received full permission from the governors of the towns where he had been. The vast profits made by the voyage had excited other merchants to undertake similar expeditions. Hawkins himself is going out again next May, and the thing needs immediate attention. I might tell the Queen that, by his own confession, he had traded in ports prohibited by your Majesty, and require her to punish him, but I must request your Majesty to give me full and clear instructions what to do." [2]

De Silva did not know what to make out of this kind of man. He must have known that a demand for punishment from the Queen, who was getting her 60 per cent, like the rest of the adventurers, would be absurd. Philip was furious. His scornful rejection of all Hawkins's entreaties when Captain Winter took that unhappy cargo of hides into Cadiz was now being repaid. "Ojo! ojo!" he wrote in exclamation opposite the name of Hawkins in De Silva's letters. Not only the Spanish, but the Portuguese, were up in arms against the daring Englishman who was treading on their privileges. He had infringed their rights by raiding negroes on the Guinea Coast. The King of Portugal made formal protest, with as much avail as the King of Spain.

There could have been no limit to Hawkins's private satisfaction with the trend of events. He found himself famous, popular, and a favourite at Court.

In spite of all Philip's anger, if Elizabeth remonstrated with the Plymouth corsair at all for what he had done in the West Indies, she knew that he understood her motives and knew where her sympathies were. He had done a very valuable service to the English marine by showing the way to the West Indies; if he terrorised Philip at the same time, Elizabeth might protest with her lips, but she rejoiced in her heart. And equally did every English Protestant rejoice. Hawkins had got even with Philip in the matter of the hides at Cadiz. He was very soon to show what his temper was in some other matters.

The affairs of the second voyage having been settled satisfactorily by the end of the year, the captain returned home to organise another. This time his boy Richard was between five and six years of age, beginning to take a keen interest in ships and the sea and maritime adventure, in the stories his mother and his Uncle William had to tell not only of his father's voyages, but of stirring deeds which were being done on their ships in all the seas. William and John Hawkins between them now owned a fleet of thirty vessels, and there was no branch of trade, there was no sort of enterprise current, in which they were not engaged. Just now one of their captains had got into trouble somehow with the Danish authorities. In February, 1566, the King of Denmark returned to John Hawkins a ship of his, together with the goods on board her, that had been "confiscated by law." There was much sympathy between the English port of Plymouth and the French port of La Rochelle. The Huguenot city armed ships for the harassing of the Catholic trade between Spain and Flanders; the Devonshire harbour received them with open arms, and the Devonshire men — chief among them William Hawkins — helped them to dispose of the loot. John was actively engaged in these operations.

For various reasons at this busy time, the sailing of the expedition to the West Indies was delayed till October, and the pertinacity of De Silva, acting on the instructions of Philip, took some effect in the interval. When things were almost ready, Hawkins received a command from the Queen forbidding him to traffic at places in the West where foreign trade was prohibited by the King of Spain. Before he should sail he was required to execute a bond in £500 not to send the *Swallow* to any port "privileged" by Philip. Hawkins did as he was told, deciding to bide his time; the bond was signed on the 31st of October. The affair was likely to be too milk-and-watery for his taste, and he sent a deputy in charge of it, himself remaining at Plymouth.

The incident is a strange one, in the light of what we know of Elizabeth's attitude towards him. Its explanation is to be found in the influence of Cecil. The saturnine Secretary of State, though in later years he found the fate and policy of England bound up with the Protestant cause, never took a personal part in the religious strife of the period; and at this time he was strongly opposed to the illicit warfare of the privateers. It offended his sense of international justice and national interest; and it was he who secured the Queen's approval of the prohibition; it was in his hand that the command was sent to

Hawkins at Plymouth. The captain sent the *Swallow* alone on a successful but undistinguished voyage, and himself waited upon events. The *Jesus of Lubek* was brought round to the Devonshire port, and Hawkins became Admiral of the Queen's ships there, remaining in that position while he concocted the plans for his third and most famous voyage, which began in 1567.

During this period of waiting occurred the incident, already related, of Hawkins's insistence upon Spanish respect for the English flag. The process by which the gunner of the *Jesus of Lubek* "lact" the Spanish admiral through and through was effective enough; when the same squadron, returning from Flanders, met the English fleet in the Channel, sent to escort the Donna Anna Maria through English waters, Philip's ships "were constrained to vayle their flags, and to acknowledge that which all must do that pass through the English seas." The affair occasioned a great disturbance, however. In the hubbub caused by the firing some Protestant prisoners on the Spanish ships escaped and boarded the *Jesus.* Hawkins liberated them. When the news reached London, Cecil was almost as enraged as Philip himself might have been. He sent down a commissioner to examine the evidence on the spot. Hawkins rested secure in the knowledge that the Spaniards had broken the laws of the port of which he was Admiral, and had shown contempt for the Queen's Majesty. He knew that Elizabeth would uphold him, even against Cecil. De Silva waxed eloquent on the grievance:

"Your mariners rob our subjects on the sea, trade where they are forbidden to go, and fire upon our ships in your harbours. Your preachers insult my master from their pulpits, and when we remonstrate we are answered with menaces. We have borne so far with their injuries, attributing them rather to temper and bad manners than to deliberate purpose. But, seeing that no redress can be had, and that the same treatment of us continues, I must consult my Sovereign's pleasure. For the last time, I require your Majesty to punish this outrage at Plymouth, and preserve the peace between the two realms."

It reads very like an ultimatum; but Philip was in no position then to send an ultimatum to England, and all the parties knew it. Hawkins went on with his plans, undisturbed by the inquiries of Cecil and the indignation of Philip; and the Queen assisted him even more fully than in 1564.

[1] Sparke.   [2] Froude: "English Seamen."

Chapter VIII - The Affair of San Juan

We now approach that third voyage of John Hawkins across the Western Ocean, which has been described as the most important expedition so far undertaken by the English nation beyond the coasts of Europe. "It was the first occasion on which English keels furrowed that hitherto unknown sea, the Bay of Mexico." Hawkins himself left a very brief narrative of an enterprise disastrous in its incidents, but full of momentous results for the history of the world.

Now appeared upon the scene of strife between Plymouth sailors and Spaniards a figure that was to be the centre of many a crowded canvas in after years — Francis Drake. From the melancholy failure of the expedition, from the unspeakable treachery of San Juan de Ulloa, dates the implacable hatred which Drake bore throughout his life against the power of Philip. He was now for the first time actively associated with his kinsman and elder, Hawkins. Born at Tavistock, he was a Devon man; but his father removed eastward while Francis was a boy. First he became chaplain of the fleet at Chatham, and afterwards vicar of Upnor on the Medway. Young Drake was brought up in a salt atmosphere, and from the earliest days of recollection all his interests were among the sailors and the ships. He was the eldest of a long family, and his father was a poor man; accordingly, the chance offering of an apprenticeship to a master-mariner of the neighbourhood was eagerly accepted, and we may be sure that it was to the taste of the apprentice. His diligence and his innate skill of seamanship were remarkable; so high did he mount in favour that his employer, a bachelor, bequeathed his ship to the boy.

Thus at a very early age Drake was trading on his own account. He had already acquired money, much experience, and knowledge of the Guinea Coast when he and Hawkins came together. Hawkins's great achievements and successes in opening up the West India trade were, of course, the theme of all sea-faring men; and no less on the Medway than in the western ports. In 1567, when the third voyage was preparing, Drake was fired with emulation, and willingly seized the opportunity of joining Hawkins. He sold his ship, bought the *Judith,* and went round to Plymouth to take his place in the flotilla. Thus, under the patronage of Hawkins, did Drake enter upon those larger adventures in distant waters which were to make him famous.

We should not forget that in all these ventures there was more than one inspiration. It was not only trade and fortune that operated with the mariners. They were Protestants, and hated the system represented by the religion and the power of Spain; every one of them took the same fierce delight as Hawkins in striking it a blow wherever they could. De Silva had full information of Hawkins's movements, and knew that this was the most formidable enterprise of the sort ever equipped in England. He warned Philip. The King of Spain made preparations to receive the adventurers in the West Indies if they should appear there, while other machinations were set on foot to prevent the expedition from starting. It appears from a letter written by Hawkins to the Queen a fortnight before he left that he had entered into an agreement with certain Portuguese to assist him — probably in the business of obtaining negroes on the Guinea Coast; but at the last moment they deserted him, either of their own motion or impelled by some extraneous influence. There was some talk of abandoning the expedition. Hawkins would not hear of it. His own words are the best evidence of the state of affairs. He wrote on September 16th that "certain Portyngales," who had made large promises and been well entertained at Plymouth, had that day fled, taking passage into France. Nevertheless, without their help, he thought he had sufficient force to carry out the project and to bring home a profit of forty thousand marks, "without the offence of the lest of any of your highnes alyes or friends." He continued: —

"It shall be no dishonour unto your highnes that your owne servante and subjecte shall in such an extremitie convert such an enterpryse and turn it both to your highnes honor and to the benefit of your whole realme which I will not enterpryse withowt your highnes consent, but am ready to do what service by your Matie shall be commanded; yet to shew your highnes the truth I should be undone if your Ma^'e should staye the voyadge, whereunto I hope your highnes will have some regard. The voyadge I pretend is to lade negroes in Genoya and sell them in the west Indyes in troke of golde perrels and esmeraldes, whereof I dowte not but to bring home great abondance to the contentation of your highnes and to the releife of a nomber of worthy servi[t]ures ready nowe for this pretended voyadge which otherwise would shortly be dryven to great misery and reddy to commit any folly. Thus having advertysed your highnes the state of this matter do most humbly praye your highnes to signifye your pleasure by this bearer which I shall most willingly accomplish."

It would, of course, have been a serious loss to Hawkins and to those who were venturing with him if the scheme had been dissipated. Men had been brought from all parts of the country to join, and the Mayor and Commonalty of Plymouth would have been faced with a very pretty problem if the three hundred or more mariners and adventurers collected there ready to sail had been suddenly disbanded. But there was never any danger; Hawkins's "Sovereyne Ladye and Good Mistresse" signified her pleasure in the manner he desired, and the fleet sailed on October 2nd. The ships he had collected in Plymouth harbour were six in number. They were:

The *Jesus of Lubek,* the royal ship of the previous voyage, Hawkins's flagship, 700 tons; master, Robert Barret; complement, 1 80. Her armament consisted of the following brass ordnance: two whole culverins, two cannons, five demi-culverins, three sacres, and two falcons; and the following iron ordnance: three demi-culverins, five sacres, two whole slings, ten fowlers, and thirty bases. For ammunition she carried fifty-four barrels of gunpowder and an equivalent supply of ball.

The *Minion,* also a royal ship; captain, John Hampton; master, John Garret, of Hampton, a Plymouth captain; Raleigh said that he was a seaman of "the greatest experience in England."

The *Swallow,* 100 tons, one of Hawkins's own ships, already mentioned as having been returned to him by the Danish Government; well-armed.

The *Angel,* 32 tons.

The *William and John;* captain, Thomas Bolton; master, James Raunce.

The *Judith,* 50 tons; captain, Francis Drake.

The first three were vessels of considerable calibre; the others insignificant as a fighting force. Ill-starred from the first, the voyage of this armada ended in the lurid horror of San Juan, every awful incident of which the Englishmen had in their minds years afterwards when they harried King Philip's galleons through thc Channcl and into the North Sea.

They set sail out of Plymouth Sound on a fine day, with hopes running high, and directed their course, as usual, for the Canary Islands. Storm took them after seven days at sea, forty leagues north of Cape Finisterre. The hurricane lasted nearly a week, during which time the fleet was separated. The boats were washed from their decks, and the *Jesus* was so stricken that it was thought impossible she could continue the voyage. Hawkins had some thought of returning to Plymouth to refit. Indeed, he had put about and shaped a course for home when, on the 11th, the weather improved, with a fair wind. They then resumed their original intention of keeping rendezvous at the Canaries with the *William and John* and the *Swallow,* which had been lost sight of. At Grand Canary, Hawkins heard that they were at Gomera, whither he repaired, and watered and victualled his ships. Thence, with a re-constituted fleet, and everything in good order, he set sail for Cape Blanc, taking it out of his "certayne Portyngales" on the way by capturing a Portuguese fishing boat and appropriating her catch of mullet. From Cape Blanc they proceeded to Cape de Verde, arriving on the 18th November.

An incident had now occurred which is somewhat obscure. One of the best narratives of the voyage, affording more detail than that of Hawkins himself, is that of Job Hortop. It was published as a pamphlet in 1591 under the title of "The Rare Travels of Job Hortop, an Englishman, who was not heard of, in three and twenty years' space. Wherein is declared the dangers he escaped in his Voyage to Guinea," etc., etc. We shall hear of him later on. Hortop gives the only description extant of the addition to the fleet of a ship which was afterwards rechristened the *Grace of God,* and took part in the great fight at San Juan. "In our course thither" (*i.e.* to Cape de Verde) "we met a Frenchman of Rochelle, called Captain Bland, who had taken a Portuguese caravel, whom our Vice-Admiral chased and took. Captain Drake, now Sir Francis Drake, was made Master and Captain of the caravel." Bland remained with the expedition. Likely enough, as he was a man from Rochelle, he was not unwilling; he may even have been known to Hawkins. At any rate, he did good service when Hawkins was hard pressed at San Juan.

At Cape de Verde the slave-hunting began. Hawkins landed 150 men. They were not very successful. They captured a few negroes, but had stiff fighting for their prey with savages who used poisoned arrows. Hawkins himself, Captain Dudley and eight men were wounded in this affair by the envenomed barbs.

"Although in the beginning" (says Sir John) "they seemed to be but small hurts, yet there hardly escaped any that had blood drawn of them, but died in strange sort, with their mouths shut some ten days before they died, and after their wounds were whole. Where I myself had one of the greatest wounds, yet, thanks be to God! escaped."

Hawkins and Dudley were the only two of the ten that recovered. The eight men died. One of the captured negroes showed the Admiral how to cure himself of the wound by drawing out the poison with a clove of garlic.

Withdrawing from this inhospitable and unprofitable region, they passed along the coast of Guinea, sending boat parties up the rivers in search of blacks. They had many adventures in the nature of skirmishes with the natives and fights with wild beasts, one of their boats being crunched up by a hippopotamus. On January 12th, 1568, they arrived at Sierra Leone. Up to that time they had taken only 150 negroes. This was poor business. It would not pay them to cross the Atlantic with such a meagre cargo, and Hawkins was about to depart for El Mina to trade for gold when his aid was sought by the representatives of one negro tribe at war with another. Three chiefs were besieging the town of Taggarin (which Hawkins had visited three years before) with an army reputed to number 50,000 men. Knowing his business at the Coast, they bargained with him for his assistance, promising that he should have as many slaves as his ships could carry from among the prisoners of war if he would take the town for them. The idea was approved. The place was strongly fortified with palisades. At first Hawkins sent up only a small force under one of the captains. The assault failed, and the Englishmen lost six killed and forty wounded. The reverse stirred up the Admiral's fighting spirit, and he took reinforcements and led them himself, attacking Taggarin "by land and sea," the pinnaces going up the estuary and using their small guns. With the aid of ball and fire and sword, they made a breach in the palisade, charged through it, and occupied the town, the inhabitants taking flight. His negro allies did the rest.

In this fight the English took about two hundred and fifty prisoners, and their friends the native chiefs secured some six hundred. Hawkins had been promised that he should have the pick of the bunch, and that was the reason which operated with him in undertaking the rather distasteful and hazardous work. "But," as he says, "the negro (in which nation is seldom or never found the truth) meant nothing less." Indeed, on the very night succeeding the engagement the chiefs struck camp and disappeared, prisoners and all. The Englishmen had therefore to rest contented with the human booty they had captured for themselves. Hortop throws a little light on the character of the native fighting, and the tender mercy which the victor displayed for the vanquished; he states that the attacking party drove 7,000 of the defenders into the sea at low water at a point where there was no help for them, and they were all drowned in the ooze.

Hawkins gathered his men, mustered his prisoners, and went back to the ships. Having watered, he proceeded to Rio Grande. In the river there the foremost ships of the English fleet were challenged by the Portuguese, who had seven caravels. The *Angel* and the *Judith*, which had gone in with the two pinnaces, were found nothing loth to fight, and drove the Portuguese vessels ashore, where their crews took to flight, carrying their negroes with them. The conflict was continued next day, when Drake, with Captain Dudley and his soldiers, landed and encountered opposition from the natives. The English lost one man in the fight, and burned the town by way of reprisal.

At the close of the operations on this coast, Hawkins had collected between four and five hundred slaves, and decided to tarry no longer. It had not been a highly satisfactory voyage so far, since the early difficulties and the opposition of the Portuguese had occasioned much delay and more fighting than he wanted. Having watered and provided his ships with fuel, he sailed once more "over the ocean sea" to the Spanish Main. The indifferent luck with which he had met ever since" he left Plymouth did not improve. The voyage across the Atlantic was long and tedious, with contrary winds and storms. Leaving Rio Grande on February 3rd, he did not sight Dominica till March 27th — forty-five days. By that time they were in sore need of water and provisions, and, as usual, the fleet remained some time at anchor off the island while they replenished. Then they sailed to Margarita, following out very much the same programme as on the previous occasion.

King Philip's proscription of all traffic with the Englishmen was no less severe than before; the desire of the Spanish settlers to trade was no less keen, and the mind of Hawkins to trade with them no less determined. Difficulties destined to end in dire disaster soon began to accrue. At Margarita, and again at Burboroata, they traded in spite of the authorities, and did very good business. They were at Burboroata two months. But when they reached Rio de la Hacha they found the situation somewhat altered during the two years that had elapsed since their last visit. The Spanish authorities were not to be bluffed or coerced so easily this time. Hawkins sent on the *Angel* and the *Judith* in front of the main body of the fleet. They had barely dropped anchor in front of the town before they received their baptism of fire. Three pieces spoke from a battery on shore, which "we requited with two of ours, and shot through the Governor's house." It was an inauspicious opening of business negotiations. The two little ships found themselves in a rather warm place, for Rio de la Hacha had been well armed and fortified since 1565; and they weighed and drew out of range. The Spaniards wasted a good deal of ammunition in the effort to get at them, but they rode smilingly at anchor for five days, awaiting the coming of Hawkins himself.

All the West was now alive with the portentous news that Achines de Plimua was among the islands again with a more formidable force than before. From Santo Domingo the Viceroy sent a dispatch-boat with papers for the Governor at La Hacha. This provided a diversion for the *Angel* and the *Judith*, which chased the unfortunate caravel in shore, and then fetched him out from under the very noses of two hundred harquebusiers. Then, satisfied with their week's work, they dropped anchor again, and kept a look-out for the Admiral.

Hawkins found the situation strained when he arrived, and took strong measures, which became stronger and stronger till, at San Juan de Ulloa, he was involved in war at close quarters with the whole strength of the Spanish fleet in those waters.

Chapter IX - The Affair of San Juan *(continued)*

So far as the actual fighting was concerned, Rio de la Hacha was a comparatively small affair. But it was a warning of what was to come. It foreshadowed the carnage of San Juan. At La Hacha there was no sufficient Spanish force to deal with the determined Englishmen, for the military material at the command of the Spaniards was poor stuff, the settlers were friendly, and the Treasurer was not averse from doing a little business under the rose. Still, Hawkins was a man of prescience, and he could not have missed the lesson that whenever he happened to be faced by a superior Spanish force he would get rough treatment. He would thus obviously refrain from provoking hostilities. It was, in fact, only by an accident that he was involved in the fight at San Juan. He had often given stress of weather as his excuse for appearing in places where King Philip did not want him; it was stress of weather without the aid of any inventive excuse that drove him to the doom of his expedition.

At Rio de la Hacha Hawkins learnt from his forerunners in the *Angel* and the *Judith* of the posture of affairs. His own first attempts to open negotiations with the Treasurer were rudely rebuffed. Since 1565 the place had been strengthened by the construction of forts in which guns were mounted, commanding all the sea approach. There were also the harquebusiers. Hawkins's old friend the Treasurer entertained the ingenious notion that he might carry out the Viceroy's orders not to trade with the Englishmen, and at the same time secure the coveted slaves, by forbidding him to land at all. Then famine of water was only a question of time, and the negroes would certainly fall into his hands.

"Of which purpose he had not greatly failed unless we had by force entered the town." Hawkins used all the civil arguments he could, and, finding them impotent, landed two hundred men. Forts, harquebusiers, and all the display of force then proved unavailing. The Spaniards hardly showed fight. Hawkins broke through the defences with perfect ease, put the enemy to flight, and occupied the town with the loss of only two men, "and no hurt done to the Spaniards; because after their volley of shot discharged they all fled." The Admiral now held the key of the situation, and turned it to good purpose. The Treasurer's "friendship" was privately secured, and as the Spanish settlers who were anxious to buy Hawkins's negroes came down to do the traffic by night, he could not be expected to see or know what was going on. Hawkins sold about two hundred slaves and disposed of other merchandise, so that when he was ready to leave La Hacha, he had nearly cleared his cargo. The landing was accomplished about the middle of June. At the beginning of July, Hawkins wished his friends good-bye, and weighed for Cartagena, carrying with him a "vast treasure" of gold, silver, and jewels.

It was the custom to store all the receipts of the traffic on board the flagship *Jesus,* and it may be interesting at this point to estimate the value of her cargo. In the course of the inquiry held by the Admiralty into the affair of San Juan, evidence was given by William Clarke, one of the four supercargoes appointed by Sir William Garrard and other adventurers in the expedition to look after their interests. He was on board the *William and John,* which was separated from the rest of the fleet during a storm, and was not, therefore, present at San Juan. His story of the transactions, however, squares with that of Hawkins himself. Gold in bars and pieces, silver plate, and other commodities to the value of 29,743 pesos, or about £11,897 of English money (which would now represent somewhere about £100,000) were on the *Jesus* after she left Cartagena.

Hawkins would have traded at Cartagena, but "the Governor was...strait" in his interpretation of the King's prohibition. This would not have weighed very heavily with the Admiral but for two additional facts: (1) Cartagena was very strongly fortified, and he could not have reduced it to submission, if at all, except at a great cost in lives and time; (2) the season of storms, "the which they call Furicanos," was approaching, and he wanted to get out of the Caribbean Sea before it came on. He therefore chose to consider the adventure closed, and departed from Cartagena on the 24th July. He had not wasted much time there. He wanted provisions, and, being unable to bring the Governor to a reasonable frame of mind, he fired a mere shot or two from the *Minion* at the castle in order to cover his movements, landed a party on one of the islands to the south-west of the town, where they had "many gardens," raided a cave where certain *botijos* of wine were stored, and left in exchange a quantity of woollen and linen cloth. Much to the distaste of the Governor as these proceedings might be, they were probably quite to the liking of the proprietors of the wine, so that no great harm was done.

His intended route from the Spanish Main to England was the same as in 1565. He set a course from Cartagena north-west to the Yucatan Channel, passing by the western end of Cuba, proposing to navigate the Straits of Florida and pass into the Atlantic. But, owing to the delays at Burboroata and La Hacha, he was too late to avoid the cyclones of August.

"Passing by the west of Cuba, towards the coast of Florida, there happened to us on the 12th day of August an extreme storm, which continued by the space of four days; which did so beat the *Jesus* that we cut down all her higher buildings; her rudder was also sore shaken, and withal she was in so extreme a leak, that we were rather upon the point to leave her than to keep her any longer."

The ships had been at sea ten months, and were not in the best condition for meeting a severe gale. Their bottoms were foul and they sailed badly. On the 15th August, after three days of beating about the entrance to the Gulf, the *William and John* was separated from the other six ships, and thought to be lost. In the event she escaped through the Straits of Florida, and arrived on the coast of Ireland in the following February. Hawkins was sorely beset, and, as his own narrative quoted above shows, strongly tempted to abandon the *Jesus.* But the great Queen's ship was valuable — worth £5,000 without counting any of her precious cargo — and a seaman of the quality of Hawkins would let no effort be lacking to save her. He led his storm-tossed fleet to the inner coast of Florida, and beat up and down to find some haven where they might repair the ship and succour their crews. The coast was shoal and perilous, no harbour was to be found, a fresh storm descended, and endured three days; and in despair the Admiral put about and fled before it to the bottom of the Gulf. And this was "the first occasion on which English keels had furrowed the waters of the Bay of Mexico." He ran straight for San Juan de Ulloa, then the port from which the City of Mexico was served, a voyage of about a thousand miles from the Floridan coast.

The amazement and wrath of the Spaniards there at his temerity in sailing the forbidden seas, and the difficulties he was likely to encounter in his endeavour to refit and provision, were foreseen by far-sighted Hawkins. On the way he met with three small Spanish vessels carrying passengers, took them, and carried them along with him; they would give him something valuable to barter with. If he could by no other means obtain his desires, he would hold them to ransom, and he did not doubt that they would greatly assist his argument. On one of the ships, bound for Hispaniola, they found a distinguished Spaniard, Augustin de Villa Nueva, "who," says Hortop, "was the man that betrayed all the noblemen in the Indies and caused them to be beheaded." Of this worthy, Hawkins, in pursuance of his policy, made a great deal, and treated him with much courtesy, the which was afterwards rewarded as might have been expected by a gentleman with such a reputation: "he was one of them that betrayed us."

Hawkins, with his five English ships, his caravel the *Grace of God,* and the three little vessels he had just captured, made a brave display as he sighted the coast of Mexico, and felt about for the port of San Juan de Ulloa. It was the chief port of the great colony, an honour it afterwards resigned to Vera Cruz, only a few miles away. Indeed, the harbour of Vera Cruz, at the present day still the principal port of Mexico, is protected by a breakwater stretched between the island of San Juan and that of Los Sacrificios. San Juan had a tiny harbour, protected by a shingle bar forming an island across the front of a little bay nestled in the south-western corner of the Golfo de Campéche. The inside edge of the island, some half-mile long, had been faced with masonry, and to this quay shipping tied up and lay in safety from the prevailing north winds which constantly rolled a long line of white surf against the outer edge. Only one of the entrances to the bay was practicable for ships of anything but very shallow draught, and this narrow gut could be commanded by guns mounted on shore. If the Spaniards had chosen to prevent any ship from entering the harbour, it was the easiest thing in the world to do, and there was no safe riding-place outside.

San Juan de Ulloa, then, it will be seen, was a particularly choice spot for the English Admiral to select who had been fighting the Spanish authorities ever since he entered these seas, and was under the ban of King Philip. It would have been a thousand times better for John Hawkins, as things turned out, if he had never gone near San Juan. But let us witness his arrival from the shore.

There was no great Spanish force in the port; twelve rich merchantmen, reported to have £200,000 in bullion on board, were there at anchor, and they were defended only by the guns on shore; no ships of war were in harbour. The local authorities were therefore looking out somewhat eagerly for the fleet from Spain, of whose approach they had been advised. It was a formidable force of galleons and frigates, under the command of the well-known Alvarez de Baçan, and its most distinguished passenger was Don Enriquez, recently appointed to supersede the Viceroy of Mexico. When, on September 16th, a squadron of nine ships appeared off the port, the local authorities were excessively relieved. The ships entered the harbour one after the other, and took up their positions along the wall of the island, and were received with the usual courtesies. When the fleet was disposed, the chief officer of San Juan went in state to the flagship, expecting to be received by de Bagan and to pay his duty to Don Enriquez. Instead, he found himself on the deck of the *Jesus of Lubek,* and was received by no less a personage than "Achines de Plimua," the pest of the Spanish Main, the corsair and enemy of the faith whom de Baçan had special instructions to find and to destroy.

"Being deceived of their expectation," they "were greatly dismayed." Hawkins had a terrible character all along the coast, and the unfortunate governor hardly knew what to expect. But, happily for him, Hawkins was not in fighting trim nor in fighting mood. He had been sorely battered in the storm; he merely wanted victuals and a quiet place in which to repair damages. Consequently, his friends the Spaniards were easily reassured. He left nothing undone, however, that might conduce to his safety and prove his intention of honest dealing. The people at San Juan were but minor personages, and Hawkins took steps at once to inform the Viceroy at Mexico of his arrival and the reason for his presence. His courier rode away inland the same evening, bearing word that Hawkins had been driven into his port by the violent weather and the necessity for repairing his ships. He pointed out that Queen Elizabeth was an ally of King Philip, and that arrangements ought to be made to prevent any rupture of friendly relations upon the arrival of the Spanish fleet which his friends at the coast informed him was daily expected.

Once more it must be pointed out that the unofficial Spaniards in the colonies had no ill-feeling for Hawkins, but regarded him rather as a benefactor than otherwise, because he brought them commodities of which they were in need. The hostility was purely official, and it did not extend even to all the officials, as we have seen in the case of the Treasurer at La Hacha. There was a possibility, then, that the Viceroy in Mexico would have winked at what had happened before, and given Hawkins licence to repair his ships and clear peaceably. But the expedition had been dogged by ill-luck ever since it left Plymouth, and Nemesis did not desert it now. Hawkins was not aware of the fact that the Viceroy was about to be succeeded by Don Enriquez, and that he was impotent to put any friendly feelings into practice. Even had this not been the case, Hawkins would have been no better off, because Nemesis closed with him before his courier was so much as a day's journey on the road to Mexico.

The Admiral had acted with great circumspection. His leading idea just now was to conciliate the authorities. The treasure-ships in the harbour were a great temptation: he announced his intention of leaving them severely alone. The passengers whom he carried — the yield of the three caravels he had captured on his way through the gulf — would have been valuable as hostages; he set them at liberty "without the taking from them the weight of a groat." His actual business of trading was over: he wanted to do nothing that might be a cause of dispute between him and the Spaniards. Throughout this episode he played quite fairly: he was met by nothing but treachery.

It was two hundred miles from San Juan to Mexico, and Hawkins's messenger could not have been far on the way when, the next morning-, "which was the seventeenth day of the same month, we saw open of the haven thirteen great ships." Alvarez de Bagan had arrived, and, lying off the port, was immensely surprised to find the harbour occupied by English vessels, and the masts of the *Jesus of Lubek* towering high above the protecting island. It was "a little island of stones not three feet above the water in the highest place, and but a bowshot of length anyway. This island standeth from the mainland two bow-shots or more. Also it is to be understood that there is not in all this coast any other place for ships to arrive in safety, because the north wind hath there such violence that, unless the ships be very safely moored, with their anchors fastened upon this island, there is no remedy for the north winds but death. Also, the place of the haven was so little that of necessity the ships must ride one aboard the other, so that we could not give place to them nor they to us."

While de Baçan, seeing that the posture of affairs was difficult, anchored his fleet outside, Hawkins revolved in his mind the procedure he should adopt. He was ever prompt in action and quick to see the key of a situation. In this case, possession of the island was the master key: from it the occupant could dictate terms to any force, however large, desiring to enter the port. He first landed a number of his men there and got guns into position covering the only practicable channel. Then he was ready to negotiate with de Baçan. Hawkins had two alternatives. He could, if he chose, prevent the Spanish fleet from entering the port, which would have been the safer course for himself, though it would have been a definite act of war; if he had prevented their ingress, they must either have departed to some other port or have been driven ashore and wrecked in the first breeze that rose. That would have been despoiling King Philip of property estimated to be worth near two millions sterling, and Hawkins feared "the Queen's indignation in so weighty a matter." He could, on the other hand, let them in, and chance their conduct afterwards; the likelihood of fair dealing he believed to be small, but he decided to run the risk. "I thought it rather better to abide the jutt of the uncertainty than the certainty. The uncertain doubt, I accounted, was their treason, which by good policy I hoped might be prevented; and therefore, as choosing the least mischief, I proceeded to conditions."

The negotiations between the two commanders lasted three days. De Baçan had not long been anchored when he sent in a pinnace with a flag of truce asking of what country those ships were that rode in the King of Spain's port. Hawkins replied that they were the, Queen of England's ships, come in there for victuals and necessaries for which they were able and willing to pay. The conversation by deputy was young when the English Admiral received information that Don Enriquez was on board, that he had authority in all the province of Mexico, in New Hispania, "and in the sea." This last was the assertion of a doctrine which it had been the invariable custom of English seamen to deny; but since the Viceroy spoke him fair in other respects, Hawkins allowed it to pass. Don Enriquez asked him to send his conditions, "which, of his part, should (for the better maintenance of amity between the Princes) be both favourably granted and faithfully performed." Much more of a complimentary kind was said. Don Enriquez was outside and in danger of being cast ashore; Hawkins had the whip-hand of him while his ships were in the harbour and his guns were on the island. The Don was suave and polite; he mentioned that passing along the coasts of the Indies, he had been informed of the honest behaviour of the Englishmen towards the inhabitants with whom they had business — "the which," says Hawkins, sententiously, "I let pass." He knew full well, remembering what had happened at Burboroata and Rio de la Hacha, that the Viceroy had his tongue in his cheek while he spoke, and was only anxious to get inside the harbour in safety. Hawkins proceeded to draw up conditions, in which the English demanded:

"Victuals for our money, and hcence to sell as much wares as would furnish our wants.

"That there might be, of either part, twelve gentlemen as hostages for the maintenance of peace.

"That the island, for our better safety, might be in our possession during our abode there, and such ordnance as was planted in the same island, which were eleven pieces of brass.

"And that no Spaniard might land in the island with any kind of weapon."

Don Enriquez and de Baçan remained polite; but they did not like Hawkins's demands, and, as events proved, had no intention of conceding them except in appearance. It was not, in fact, at all likely that the Spanish Admiral, who had instructions so rigid with regard to Hawkins and his company, would let him slip now that they were at close quarters and the Spaniards in overwhelming force. Some demur was made about the provision that the island should remain in the hands of the English; but it was, as already set forth, the key of the situation, without which the English fleet would not have been worth half an hour's purchase. The island in their possession, it would have been the simplest thing in the world for the Spaniards to have cut the cables and Hawkins's ships would infallibly have gone ashore against the town of San Juan. At last, at the end of three days, Don Enriquez concluded the treaty, granting all Hawkins's conditions, except that the number of the hostages was reduced to ten on each side. The Viceroy signed the papers on his part, and sealed them with his seal; and forthwith a trumpet was sounded, "with the commandment that none, of either part, should be means to violate the peace, on pain of death." Then Hawkins and de Baçan met with formal ceremony, and gave personal pledge of the performance of their promises.

So the stately galleons and frigates of the Spanish fleet made an impressive procession into the little harbour, amid the firing of complimentary salutes on either side, and a great deal of powder smoke, "as the manner of the sea doth require." This was at night on Monday, the 20th of September. Up to this time there had been no cause of complaint of any breach of the conditions, except that suspicions arose that the Spanish hostages were not the genuine article, but varlets dressed up in fine apparel to look like gentlemen. The tiny harbour was inconveniently crowded; there were the twelve treasure-ships, the nine that Hawkins had brought in, and the thirteen of the Spanish fleet — altogether thirty-four sail. It took them two days to sort themselves out and get the two fleets moored in two separate bunches. While this work was a-doing, the officers and men on both sides fraternised freely, from the captains to the scullions. So passed Tuesday and Wednesday.

While Hawkins was busying himself about arrangements for the repair of his ships, and while his crews were hobnobbing with the Spaniards of the fleet, Don Enriquez, Admiral de Baçan, and the Governor of San Juan were ashore deliberating upon the means of scotching, if not of killing, the pernicious Englishman. They prepared an attack for Thursday, which was meant to be resistless. With a less wide-awake man than Hawkins, and with more pusillanimous material than he had at his command, their plan would have been a perfect success. They had gathered a thousand armed men at San Juan, and had completed the scheme for assisting their operations by the fire of their ships. They had their spy, Augustin de Villa Nueva, on board the *Jesus* with a knife in his sleeve. They had 300 men on a hulk ready to board the *Minion.* If this did not succeed, it argued ill for their capacity for secret plotting. This was the posture of affairs when night closed down upon the Bay of San Juan on Wednesday.

Chapter X - The Affair of San Juan *(concluded)*

Though the fight at San Juan was not on the grand scale as sea-fights go, it was one of the most desperate in naval history. In some other respects it was notable. All the fighting was at close quarters; the destruction and the carnage were great in proportion to the size of the forces engaged.

When Thursday morning broke, signs of feverish activity were seen on shore and on board the Spanish ships. Guns were being shifted and trained on the little island, parties of men-at-arms were mustered here and there, and boat-loads of them were passing and repassing between ship and shore. These things aroused "a vehement suspicion." Hawkins took the bull by the horns. He sent a message to the Spanish flagship to inquire what was afoot. It proved that, though the great ship next the *Minion* had been filled with men, though in the night a hawser had been fastened to the head cable of the *Jesus* where she rode, and there seemed not to be the slightest loophole of escape for the English, caught like rats in a trap, the Spaniards were not yet ready to strike, and the Viceroy, to disarm the doubts of the English, ordered the preparations to be masked, and sent word to Hawkins that he, on the faith of a Viceroy, would be their defence against all villainies.

The Admiral had no particular reason for relying on the faith of a Viceroy. He saw this to be mere temporising, because it had been definitely ascertained that the ship next the *Minion* had 300 men (above and beyond her crew) on board. Hawkins, hoping to get a better explanation, sent to the flagship the Master of the *Jesus,* Robert Barret, who spoke Spanish very well. Barret had instructions to demand "that those men might be unshipped again which were in that great hulk." Meanwhile, Hawkins sat at table in his stateroom with Augustin de Villa Nueva. The Admiral, sometimes represented as a rough and uncouth seaman, half pirate, kept a good table and some style. On ceremonial occasions he wore silks and velvets, elaborately ornamented with gold and pearls. We may legitimately picture him in his garb of state this fatal morning, for he regarded Villa Nueva as a person of consequence.

The symposium was rudely disturbed by the sound of a trumpet and an uproar on deck. In the state room, one John Chamberlayne, who had been watching Villa Nueva, suddenly seized him by the arm, and took from his sleeve a dagger. Hawkins leapt to his feet, faced the trembling Spaniard for a moment, sternly commanded him to be imprisoned in the steward's room and guarded by two men. Then he rushed on deck. All was in confusion. The trumpet note had been the signal for a general attack upon the English. There were shots and shrieks on shore, where parties of Hawkins's men had been overwhelmed; the Spanish ships were spitting smoke and ball from all their ports; the hawser attached to the head cable of the *Jesus* was used to haul the big hulk up alongside the *Minion,* and men poured from her decks over both the *Minion* and the flagship.

What had happened was this: when Barret went on board the Spanish flagship, he was invited to a conference with the Viceroy, and had barely delivered his message when the Spaniards perceived that it would be impossible longer to conceal their intentions. Barret and his boat's crew were seized and put in irons, and the command was given for a general assault. The first great slaughter took place on the island. Large numbers of Spaniards, armed to the teeth, scrambled ashore from the ships, and overran the place, killing right and left, and immediately capturing the battery of eleven guns which Hawkins had mounted to command the entrance to the harbour. Not an Englishman was left alive on shore; the few who survived escaped by swimming off to the *Jesus.* The stones of the island were encarmined with English blood and strewn with English corpses.

When Hawkins got on deck he found his crew much taken aback by the suddenness of the attack. He saw at once that the *Minion* must be saved, or they would be undone. "God and Saint George!" cried he. "Upon those traitorous villains and rescue the *Minion!* I trust in God, the day shall be ours!" His men only needed a lead. With a cheer they swarmed from the *Jesus* into the *Minion,* and in a fierce hand-to-hand fight beat the Spaniards back. Many returned to the hulk, many were left dead upon the Englishman's decks, and many were driven overboard and drowned. Amid the storm of fire, they got the *Minion's* guns to work, and one of their first lucky shots was fired into the Spanish Vice-Admiral's ship and set him on fire, so that presently his magazine exploded. The better part of 300 men perished in this catastrophe. The engagement waxed hotter. The Spaniards concentrated most of their fire upon the devoted *Jesus,* and she lived in a rain of chain-shot and ball. Her mainmast was pierced in five places, her foremast went by the board, and her hull was riddled, so that she was soon reduced to a helpless wreck.

After the first boarding had been repulsed, the *Minion* slipped her cable, and worked to the mouth of the harbour, firing as she went in answer to the guns on the island. The storm of iron lulled for a brief space, only to allow the boarding party from the big hulk to attack the *Jesus.* Again they were repulsed with much loss on both sides. The *Jesus* then followed the example of the *Minion,* and was warped round by her stern-fasts to the opening. But her case was hopeless, for she was almost unmanageable. The men continued to work the guns, Hawkins encouraging them. "Our General courageously cheered up his soldiers and gunners, and called to Samuel, his page, for a cup of beer, who brought it to him in a silver cup. And he, drinking to all the men, willed the gunners to stand by their ordnance lustily, like men. He had no sooner set the cup out of his hand but a demi-culverin struck away the cup and a cooper's plane that stood by the mainmast, and ran out on the other side of the ship; which nothing dismayed our general, for he ceased not to encourage us, saying, 'Fear nothing, for God, who hath preserved me from this shot, will also deliver us from these traitors and villains.'" [1]

The *Judith*, Drake's little 50-ton ship, followed out, being less damaged than the others, and got clear of the guns. The *Jesus*, however, could not be rescued; her tackle had all been destroyed by the fire. All she could do was to remain a target for the Spanish guns, and fire her own as quickly as might be. And the English guns were worked to some effect, for in addition to the destruction of the Vice-Admiral's ship, they sank de Baçan's flagship under him within an hour after the general engagement began, and three others were afterwards wrecked. But the odds were too great. When Hawkins realised that there was absolutely no possibility of saving the *Jesus*, he ordered the next best thing to be done. She was warped in front of the *Minion*, between her and the island, so as to act as a buffer for the fire from the battery, the intention being to keep up the defence till nightfall, get the treasure and as much of the stores out of her as could be taken, and slip away.

Once more there was no luck for the Admiral. His purpose was defeated by means that foreshadowed a striking incident of a much greater fight just twenty years after: "As we were thus determining, and had placed the *Minion* from the shot of the land, suddenly the Spaniards had fired two great ships, which were coming directly with us." Battered for hours by heavy gun-fire, with their comrades lying around them dead and dying, this device of the enemy was too much for them. A similar project had been entertained by the Frenchman, Captain Bland, of the *Grace of God.* He had been trying to follow the other three out of the harbour, when his mainmast crashed overboard, severed by chain-shot. He dropped anchor, set the caravel on fire, and took his men in their pinnace on board the *Jesus.*

Hawkins was frankly surprised to find him so loyal, and told him he had imagined that the *Grace of God* was attempting to escape alone. Bland replied that he had not meant to run away, but to have laid the weathermost (which would be the nearest to him) of the Spanish ships aboard, fired his ship, and trusted to that element to win the day. Hawkins commended the plan; but the immediate necessity was to escape a similar fate himself. His men were almost dead-beat with exhaustion. Whereas he (as he told the Admiralty Court) "had all that day attended to the defence of the *Jesus*, and his company by their good travail and manliness had stoutly stood unto the same defence, the sudden approaching of the fired ships made a great alteration of things." Some of the men were for an immediate escape into the *Minion*, which was in comparatively good case; others preferred waiting to see whether the fire-ships would be carried away from them by the wind. The *Minion*, without orders from Hawkins, took the problem into its own hands, made sail, and began to slip away. Hawkins, with difficulty, jumped on board her as she left the *Jesus*, most of the men then alive in the flagship followed out in a small boat, "the rest, which the little boat was not able to receive, were enforced to abide the mercy of the Spaniards; which I doubt was very little."

The *Judith* was already outside; the *Minion* dropped anchor a mile from the shore; night came down, and the Battle of San Juan de Ulloa was over. It had been eight hours of the hottest fighting; the number of Englishmen killed on

65

the island and in the ships was not less than 100, probably more; Spanish records of the affair admitted 540 killed of the 1,500 men they had in the engagement — of whom the majority were accounted for by the blowing up of the Vice-Admiral's ship.

In view of the disparity of the forces engaged, it is hardly short of marvellous that an English ship escaped at all, or that an Englishman should have been left to tell the tale — save to the officers of the Inquisition who thereafter dealt with some of the prisoners. About two hundred gallant, battle-weary men, many of them suffering torture from their wounds, were huddled on board the *Minion* and the *Judith* outside San Juan when night fell. In the morning, the Admiral and the ship's company of the *Minion* were amazed to find that they were alone; the *Judith* had disappeared. The reason why Drake sailed away, leaving his Admiral in this necessity, is not quite clear. Hawkins himself complained of desertion, and thought it was a hard case. He writes: "So with the *Minion* only, and the *Judith,* a small bark of 50 tons, we escaped; which bark, the same night, forsook us in our misery." But there is another side to the story, which shows that the apparent desertion may have been the result of a misunderstanding. Hortop relates that Hawkins "willed Master Francis Drake to come in with the *Judith,* and to lay the *Minion* aboard, to take in men and other things needful; and to go out. And so he did." Further, Phillips [2] says of the incident, "the same night the said bark lost us." It was not in concert with the character of Francis Drake that he should desert a comrade in distress, and in the absence of any other testimony it should not be assumed against him.

As soon as the *Jesus* was abandoned by the English, the Spaniards diverted their fireships and took possession of her, so that all the treasure which Hawkins had expected to be able to bring home to the Queen, Sir William Garrard, and the other adventurers, "forty thousand marks of gain," all his "golde, perrels, and esmeraldes," were fallen into the hands of the Dons. If de Bagan had been a seaman and a fighter of the calibre of Hawkins, he would have had the Admiral himself and the *Minion* as well as the treasure. The Spanish commander had several ships fit for action, while, a mile away, lay the *Minion,* which had been raked by their fire all day, and was crowded with refugees. But no further attempt upon her was made.

The next morning (September 24th) Hawkins, in melancholy case, weighed and sailed to the protection of an adjacent island — probably Los Sacrificios — where, at any rate, they were safe from the guns, and a good watch would give them timely warning of any intended attack. They had lost three cables and two anchors during the fight and the warping out, and had only two anchors and cables left, so that when the dreaded *nortes* came on, there seemed no hope of anything but shipwreck to end their troubles. However, the weather rapidly improved again, and on the Saturday (25th) they set sail.

Now began a sorrowful fortnight's wandering "in an unknown sea." The ship was crowded and ill-provisioned, for they had been able to do none of the work they expected to accomplish at San Juan. Nothing more pathetic can be imagined than Hawkins's simple language in description of their plight: "Our hope of life waxed less and less. Some desired to yield to the Spaniards. Some rather desired to obtain a place where they might give themselves to the infidels" (the Aztec Indians). "And some hath rather abide with a little pittance the mercy of God at sea."

Hunger at last drove them to land; they had eaten their mice, cats, and dogs; they had eaten the parrots and monkeys bought for pets, and, however great a price had been given for these, they were thought profitable if they served the turn of a dinner; they had begun to eat the hides in which the expedition had invested some of its gains, and these were thought very good meat. But this was a state of things in which it was madness to dream of voyaging the thousand miles to the Florida channel, and the three thousand miles across the Atlantic. On the 8th of October, they struck land on the Mexican coast some miles north of the Panuco river, which was the estuary they were seeking, with its port of Tampico. Unfortunately, they missed it and happened upon a part of the coast which was quite inhospitable and uninhabited. Their ship was leaky, and they could only just keep her afloat. So badly had she been served by the Spanish ordnance and so shaken by the firing of her own, "our weary and weak arms were scarce able to defend and keep out the water." All they found at this point was a place where they might with some difficulty send a boat ashore.

It would not be easy to imagine a more perilous fix for a commander with nearly 200 men on his hands than that in which Hawkins now found himself. It was manifestly impossible that he should take them all with him in the *Minion* on the long voyage to Europe; it was equally impossible for him to remain there with his ship or to get substantial succour in any of the Spanish ports. The men suggested the only way out. Some of them, suffering under the intolerable pangs of hunger, declared that they would rather be set on shore and left to shift for themselves as best they might, than endure any more of the privations and hardships of the *Minion,* with only this prospect in front of them, that they should presently die like flies from disease and starvation. Hawkins consented. Such as were willing to take their chance in New Spain he put on one side; such as would rather share his own fate he put on the other side. The ship's company was then divided into two nearly equal portions. In this connection, Hawkins had been most unjustly accused of abandoning his men. On this point, let Phillips speak: [3]

"Being thus oppressed with famine on the one side and danger of drowning on the other, not knowing where to find relief, we began to be in wonderful despair, and we were of many minds. Amongst whom there were a great many that did desire our general to set them on land; and making their choice rather to submit to the mercy of the savages or infidels than longer to hazard themselves at sea: where they very well saw that, if they should all remain together, if they perished not by drowning, yet hunger would enforce them, in the end, to eat one another. To which request our general did very willingly agree, considering with himself that it was necessary for him to lessen his number; both for the safety of himself and the rest."

And Phillips goes on to speak of the quarrelling that at once arose. He is a credible witness, because he was one of those who chose to land, and suffered intensely thereafter, in imprisonment, slavery, and Inquisition torture; and if Hawkins had been at fault, Phillips would have said so. Hortop, quite an independent narrator, corroborates him in this matter. As soon as the decision was taken and the division made, "it was a world to see how suddenly men's minds were altered!" Some who had just been asking to be set ashore now wanted to stay; others who had wanted to go home now desired to be set ashore. Hawkins, as usual, took the direct and commonsense course. He chose to stay with him the most necessary persons for the management of the ship; and of those who were willing to remain in the country he sent ashore those who he thought could best be spared, to the number of about a hundred. Accounts differ between 94 and 112. The farewells were painful, of course; but Hawkins promised that the next year he would either come and fetch them himself, or send for them. Before a year had passed, they had been scattered far and wide, and most of them were in Spanish prisons.

Hawkins then turned his attention to the *Minion* and the voyage home. There was no opportunity of revictualling, but they could replenish their water casks, and he landed 50 men for the purpose, himself going with them. While they were ashore, the *nortes* came on again; "there arose an extreme storm," which prevented communication with the ship for three days. Fearfully they waited for the weather to improve, every hour expecting the leaky *Minion* to be driven on this terrible lee shore. "But yet God again had mercy on us, and sent fair weather." They got the water casks on board, and sailed, with their reduced crew on short rations, on October 16th. From Tampico to Cape Sable on the southern point of the Floridan peninsula is more than a thousand miles; but they had good weather and made a quick passage, disemboguing into the Atlantic through the Bahama Channel on November 16th. The month, however, had made great inroads on their stock of provisions, and as they sailed into colder climes the famine preyed upon them severely. Many men died; those who survived were so weak that they were hardly able to work the ship. In this condition they crawled across the Atlantic. Driven by contrary winds too far south to enable him to make the channel, Hawkins was obliged to set a course for the land of his enemies. There was irony in it. He steered for Vigo, and finally on December 31st hauled into the harbour of Pontevedra, a little to the north.

England and Spain were at peace, and there was nothing to prevent Hawkins from re-victualling in a Spanish port. But news of the affair at San Juan had already reached Spain. William Hawkins, at Plymouth, on December 3rd, had received a letter from Benedick Spinola, stating that the English fleet was totally destroyed. On his arrival at Pontevedra, Hawkins would allow none of his men on shore. He had fresh meat sent off to him, of which they ate so ravenously as to produce a surfeit from which many of them died. The news spreading that "Achines de Plimua" was in port, the Spanish authorities became curious and menacing. Hawkins at once weighed for Vigo, where the chances were that he would find English ships. This expectation was not disappointed. They had help from British captains lying there, who, hearing Hawkins's sad tale, put twelve fresh men on board of him to work the ship home. He left Vigo on January 20th, 1569, and dropped anchor in Mount's Bay five days later.

"If," says Hawkins, "all the miseries and troublesome affairs of this sorrowful voyage should be perfectly written, there should need a painful man with his pen, and as great a time as he had that wrote the Lives and Deaths of the Martyrs."

The account of San Juan de Ulloa may fitly conclude with the letter written by Hawkins to Sir William Cecil the day of his arrival on the English coast: —

"Right Honorable, — My dewty most humbly consydered: yt may please your honor to be advertysed that the 25th day of Januarii (thanks be to God) we aryved in a place in Cornewall called Mounts bay, onelie with the *Minyon* which is left us of all our flet, and because I wold not in my letters be prolyxe, after what manner we came to our dysgrace, I have sent your honor here inclosed some part of the circumstance, and though not all our meseryes that hath past yet the greatest matters worthye of notynge, but yf I shold wryt of all our calamytyes I am seure a volome as great as the byble wyll scarcelie suffyce; all which things I most humblie beseeche your honor to advertyse the Queens Majestie and the rest of the counsell (soch as you shall thinke mette).

"Our voyage was, although very hardly, well achieved and brought to reasonable passe, but now a great part of our treasure, merchandyze, shippinge and men devoured by the treason of the Spanyards.

"I have not moche or any thynge more to advertyse your honor, nore the rest, because all our business hath had infelycytye, mysfortune, and an unhappy end, and therefore wyll treble the Queens Majestie nore the rest of my good lords with soch yll newes. But herewith pray your honours estate to impart to soch as you shall thynke mete the sequell of our busyness.

"I mind with God's grace to make all expedicyon to London myselfe, at what tyme I shall declare more of our (isstate that ys here omytted. Thus prayinge to God for your Honours prosperous estate take my leave: from the *Mynion* the 25th day of Januarii 1569.

"Yours most humbly to command (signed) John Hawkyns."

Hawkins sent ashore in Mount's Bay for help, and for fresh anchors and cables: he had but one left. The men had a terrible story to tell the Cornishmen — of casting forty-five dead bodies overboard, and of the rest of the crew subsisting for seven days on one oxhead. The sympathetic Englishmen did what they could on the instant, and one of them posted straightway to Plymouth, eighty miles distant, to inform William Hawkins what had befallen his brother. William had heard the story of San Juan already, and was in some doubt whether John was dead or alive. Immediately on receiving the news, he sent off a vessel from Plymouth to Mount's Bay, with victuals, anchors, cables, and other ship's necessaries; then with impatience he awaited the arrival of John himself.

[1] Hortop's Narration, in Hakluyt.
[2] See Hakluyt.
[3] See Hakluyt.

Chapter XI - Aftermath

In the house in Kinterbury Street, Plymouth, where dwelt with William Hawkins Dame Katharine and her little son Richard, now between nine and ten years of age, the seven weeks from the 3rd of December to the 25th of January had been weeks of agonising suspense. In the ordinary course of events, if John's voyage had been favourable, he would have reached home in October or November. The two months' grace might be allowed him for contingencies; but on the 3rd of December his brother received news which foreshadowed his fate. William Winter (afterwards famous in connection with Drake's circumnavigation) informed William Hawkins on that day of the letter he had received from Benedick Spinola, who had heard from Spain that in his enterprise in the Indies John Hawkins had been constrained to land, and to travel far inland in pursuit of his traffic, and that he had been entrapped and put to the sword with all his company after a desperate fight. If this were true, William wrote to Cecil, ""I should have cause to curse them Mhiles I live, and my children after me." But he had doubts about the accuracy of the report; he thought the Spaniards had probably invented it with details to their liking. There was some good ground for mistrust. We have already heard the story of the Genoese ducats, and the cock-and-bull tale that Diaz had told of Hawkins's success, how John had sacked a town and laden himself with gold and jewels. They were not duped by that story in Plymouth; they hoped Spinola's might be equally false. But the treasure-ships of Diaz were still in the harbour, and were kept there, as we have seen, till veritable news came.

The suspense continued unabated till the 22nd of January. On the evening of that day, a torn and tattered vessel entered Plymouth Sound and worked across to Cattewater. She was a stranger to the harbour. She had evidently been in the wars, for her jury-rigging and her battered hull told their own story. Her young captain was pulled to the Barbican steps and went ashore, and so to the house in Kinterbury Street. The vessel was the *Judith,* and William Hawkins's visitor was Francis Drake. He had a long and melancholy narrative to recite, but to all inquiries about John Hawkins he could return only a dubious answer. He might have escaped from San Juan — he might not. The

70

little *Judith* had been three months on the voyage from the coast of Mexico, and had troubles and sorrows of her own. All Drake could tell them, in fact, was that the expedition had been a ruinous failure through the treachery of the Spaniards, that the *Jesus* and her precious cargo had been abandoned, and that John Hawkins was on the *Minion,* anchored off the island when his kinsman last saw him.

William spent no time in sorrowful reflections. Whether his brother was dead or alive, whether the Spaniards had slain him or the sea had claimed him, he and his family were despoiled of the money and the ships they had embarked in the venture, and despoiled by Spanish villainy; Spanish treasure-ships were in Plymouth harbour; would it not be a monstrous thing to let them go without taking recompense for this disaster? That same night, while Drake was in the house, William Hawkins sat down and indited letters to Cecil and to the Privy Council, advising them of what had happened so far as he knew it, and recommending the course to be taken with regard to the ships under Diaz. These letters he confided to Drake himself, and despatched him forthwith to London.

"To the Right Honourable and my singular good Lords, the Lords of the Privy Council; give this at the Court with all speed. Haste! Haste!" So the letter to the Council was endorsed in the fashion of the time. There was no need for the formal injunction: Francis Drake had been hit himself in the misadventure of San Juan, as well as the Hawkinses, and he was darkly revolving in his own mind as he sped to London schemes for the recovery of his losses with interest. How they materialised is to be read in the story of his raid on the treasure train at Panama, and his capture of the *Cacafuego* in the Pacific.

Almost as soon as Drake could have reached London, William Hawkins at Plymouth had the other thread of the tragedy in his hand. On the 27th, the messenger from St. Michael's Mount arrived in Plymouth with the sorry news of the *Minion.* William first of all sent the succours just mentioned, and then wrote to Cecil, sending a special messenger. The decision to transfer the Genoese ducats to London had already been taken, and Sir Arthur Champernown, with a train of horse, foot, and artillery to guard it, purposed leaving Plymouth on the morrow. William then sat down to await the return of the brother whose absence was to him "more grefe than any other thing in this world"; Dame Katharine and her boy the home-coming of the husband and father whom they had feared they would never see again.

They were exciting times for Kinterbury Street, but when Hawkins came up, and Drake spread the tale in London, and the news was generally bruited about, the excitement was almost as great in every house in every other town where it became known. England was furious at the treachery of Don Enriquez and de Baçan; it gloried in the gallant fight that Hawkins had made against such odds. England cursed the Spaniards who slew a hundred of its sons in the harbour of San Juan and had now a hundred more at their mercy in New Spain; England worshipped the men who had endured this outrage, and the sufferings that were its sequel.

Spain was hated the more because its star was again in the ascendant. While the English mariners in the western seas were being blown to pieces by Spanish guns, while their survivors were being tortured and led off to slavery on Spanish plantations, the Duke of Alva was crushing the Netherlands, the Queen of Scots was in England and the centre of Catholic conspiracy; the Protestant part of England began to growl out the prelude to that great thunderstorm which culminated in the stupendous roar of 1588. The horror of San Juan, and the fate of the men whom Hawkins had left setting off on their perilous march to Tampico — these were the topics of discussion in every sea-port; everywhere Hawkins was hailed as a hero; everywhere men were ready to join him in any enterprise that he might attempt to strike once more at the power of Spain, whose only active opponent now was the privateer fleet of the Prince of Orange, in which William Hawkins held a commission. The feeling was very deep. There was good cause for it — how good the people of England did not know till years afterwards.

It may be well here to summarise shortly the adventures that befell the hundred men Hawkins had left in Mexico, and the few prisoners taken at San Juan. Their story will explain much of the growing indignation against Philip and the Inquisition, since it was the story of nearly every Englishman who chanced to fall into their hands.

We left Robert Barret, the master of the *Jesus,* in irons on board de Baçan's flagship. He was taken out of the vessel before she sank, and into the town. There he might have seen some of his unfortunate compatriots, taken when the Spaniards seized the *Jesus,* strung up to tall posts by their arms till the blood burst through the skin of their finger-tips. Some of these escaped in the end, and bore about England the marks of their torture for a witness to their words. Barret was taken to Mexico and imprisoned, shipped to Spain in 1570, dungeoned at Seville and Triana till 1573, tried by the Inquisition, and burned at the stake for a heretic. John Gilbert, who was among those landed by Hawkins, shared his fate. Job Hortop and John Bone, after serving as slaves in Mexico, were imprisoned in Spain till 1573, when they were sentenced to ten years at the galleys and subsequent imprisonment for life. Others at the same time were sent to the galleys for various terms. Hortop escaped his imprisonment after twelve years at the galleys, and, having served the Treasurer of the King's Mint two years as a menial, contrived to flee to England. Phillips, who was with another party, gives horrible details of flogging and other torture at the instance of the Holy Inquisition in Mexico.

Indignation flamed in England as tales of this sort dribbled home. Hawkins, as we shall see, left no stone unturned to secure the rescue of his men. The expedition he had promised was impracticable. It soon became known that all the English were prisoners, and that the majority of them had been sent up to the city of Mexico, where they could not be reached by force. Hawkins then turned to diplomacy. But, meanwhile, the affairs of the third voyage were still unsettled. The adventurers had a big claim to make against Spain, and Hawkins was busily engaged for some time in the inquiry by the Admiralty into the extent of the English losses. This was held in March. Depositions were made by several witnesses, including Hawkins himself, upon eleven interrogatories, and in answer to questions directed to the formation of a schedule of values, Hawkins deposed that the expedition cost; £16,500 in all to lit out, and the treasure on board the *Jesus* was nearly £12,000. His personal belongings were valued at £440, and included twelve pieces of tapestry with which his stateroom was hung.

The claim put in against Spain for all these losses was, of course, never satisfied. Philip could retort in double barrel. He could point out that in going to the West Indies at all Hawkins was transgressing the commands of the owner of those colonies. Trading with the planters by any foreigners of English or other nationality had been expressly forbidden; Hawkins had defied the fleet of Spain in a Spanish port and had paid the penalty. Nothing was said about the manner in which it was exacted. The second barrel was charged with complaints against the privateer fleet that infested the Channel, and wrought havoc among the Spanish ships carrying money and supplies to the Netherlands. This fleet, we have noted, was now the only active engine of Protestantism employed against the Roman system. Froude describes it as "the strangest phenomenon in naval history." It was compounded chiefly of English and Dutch vessels, with some Huguenot privateers. Count de la Marck, its Admiral, was a Flemish noble. Its operations were directed from the Downs or Dover Roads, but a secondary base was Plymouth Harbour, where it could refit and hide in safety when occasion demanded. The Hawkinses had several ships in it, and made large profits from the spoil of Spanish treasure. The cargoes taken

"were openly sold in Dover market. If the Spanish ambassador is to be believed in a complaint which he addressed to Cecil, Spanish gentlemen taken prisoners were set up to public auction there for the ransom they would fetch, and were disposed of for one hundred pounds each. If Alva sent cruisers from Antwerp to bum them out, they retreated under the guns of Dover Castle. Roving squadrons of them flew down to the Spanish coasts, pillaged churches, carried off church plate, and the captains drank success to piracy out of chalices. The Spanish merchants at last estimated the property destroyed at three million ducats, and they said that if their flag could no longer protect them, they must decline to make further contracts for the supply of the Netherlands Army." [1]

This sort of fierce work was exactly to the taste of John Hawkins, burning under a sense of the wickedness of San Juan; he and his seamen of the West rejoiced in taking it out of the Spaniards in kind. If Spanish gentlemen were put up to auction in Dover market, their position was undignified; but what was it compared with that of Englishmen left to the tender mercies of slave-drivers in Mexico, or brought to the *auto da fé* at Seville? The work went on, Hawkins added further laurels to his name as a seaman, and to his fame with Queen Elizabeth; but all the while he thought of the hundred comrades he had left on the beach to the north of the Panuco river, how to save them and restore them to their friends. Another expedition was impossible, and would have been useless had it been possible; Hawkins was revolving a deep plot in his mind which was put into execution two years afterwards.

Meantime, while he was not at sea, he resided at Plymouth, where his popularity was unbounded. In 1571 he and Sir Humphrey Gilbert were elected members of Parliament for the town, and proceeded to London. There he was better able to advance the design he had conceived for undoing the King of Spain and getting his comrades deliverance.

[1] Froude.

Chapter XII - The Feria Plot

It was in 1572 that Hawkins made his first essay in statecraft, and proved that in the devious ways of diplomacy and political plotting he could be no less acute, discreet, and successful than in the conduct of maritime affairs. In order to the proper understanding of the Feria conspiracy, in which Hawkins was the chief agent, it is well to take a brief view of the situation in which this proceeding was sanctioned by the Queen and by Cecil, now Lord Burleigh. Cecil had been no friend to Hawkins in the past. His influence had been cast against the expeditions to the Indies because, to him, they savoured of buccaneering. He had never concealed his dislike for adventurers of the school of Hawkins. But he had been compelled by this time to admit the importance of Hawkins as a personage in the nation, and when the Feria affair was unfolded to him he acquiesced in it. He had learnt that his quiet way would not do, and that the Spanish pretensions and the dangers at home must be fought with stronger and more subtle weapons than he had been willing to employ hitherto.

The Ridolfi conspiracy opened his eyes, and startled the country. In May, 1572, both Houses of Parliament demanded the execution of Mary Queen of Scots. Queen Elizabeth courageously and generously rejected the demand. Yet Cecil knew that if the plot had been successful, the murder of the Queen would have preceded the elevation of Mary and the extermination of heresy. This is anticipating the story; but it illustrates the gradual conversion of Cecil's mind to the necessity for sterner measures.

The air was full of plot, counterplot and suspicion at the beginning of 1572, when John Hawkins learned that a large number of his marooned seamen had been removed from Mexico to Spain, and were in the prison of the Inquisition at Seville, where they ran the risk of a mere cast of the die between the martyr's stake and the Spanish galleys. He raged in his heart at his impotence for succour. The disturbed condition of political affairs in England suggested to him a means by which he might at the same time assist the Queen against her enemies, and secure the release of those of his companions who were alive and had so far escaped the clutches of the Holy Office. What could not be done by force of arms might be achieved by guile. And, if, in the tremendous deception which gradually took practical shape in his mind, he felt any qualms of conscience, the memory of the blood-stained pebbles of San Juan Island and the corpse-strewn decks of the *Jesus of Lubek* provided a sufficient antidote.

Hawkins knew that the Spanish ambassador in London was fully informed of every move in the game which the malcontent Catholics in England were playing, and was the direct intermediary between Philip and Alva and the Duke of Norfolk. The Catholics in the Eastern Counties were to rise under Norfolk when Philip gave the word, and the Duke of Alva was to invade England from the Netherlands. Hawkins went to the ambassador for a private conversation. The representative of Spain at the English Court was Don Guerau de Espes: de Silva, the medium of so many of Philip's protests to the Queen about the illicit proceedings of "Achines de Plimua," was gone.

Hawkins found, as he expected, that the ambassador was ready to listen to any tale that accorded with his own ambitions and with the state in which he believed public opinion to be. It was an article of faith of the Spanish party that a great body of discontent existed in England, and that it was not confined to the Catholics. Under the cover of extreme secrecy, Hawkins — who had not been visiting Spanish countries all these years without acquiring something of the Castilian tongue — told Don Guerau that he and a great number of his friends were extremely dissatisfied with the treatment they were receiving from Queen Elizabeth. She was a miser; she was niggard of her money; she did not keep her promises; she did not reward the services which the volunteer fleet rendered to her; the volunteer fleet was ready to mutiny. It was a cool suggestion to make, and it would not have succeeded with a man who knew the antecedents and character of Hawkins, or was able to gauge the signs of the times in England. Hawkins would probably not have tried to work it with de Silva. Philip himself, when the matter came to his ears afterwards, showed more discrimination than his ambassador: he could not believe, until he was over-persuaded, that Hawkins was anything but a fiery Protestant, a lost heretic, and a devoted servant of his Queen.

Don Guerau, however, took it all in. Hawkins added to his complaints about his treatment by the Queen a still more daring assertion, and many ingenious arguments to persuade him of its sincerity. He professed his affection for the one true Church; he expressed his bitter lamentation over the evil deeds he had committed in the past; he said he was horrified by the strides that heresy was making in England, and that he was eager to assist in any way he could to place the Catholic Queen of Scots upon the Throne!

The idea of the Spanish ambassador sitting as Father Confessor to the arch-captain of the English privateers must have been humorous, even to stolid Hawkins; the ambassador's blindness to the ludicrous aspect of the situation showed how well Hawkins had judged his man and his hour. The best way that suggested itself to his mind, Hawkins said, for bringing about the consummation that they both desired, was that he should turn over, with his west-country fleet of privateers, to the cause of the King of Spain — if Philip would have them. All he wanted in return was the release of the poor sailors he had left upon the coast of Mexico — unfortunate mariners who knew nothing of high politics, and were not responsible for anything that had happened in the West Indies and on the Spanish Main.

Don Guerau believed his story. Many a cleverer man has believed a farrago of nonsense which chanced to be in concert with his own wishes. It was necessary for the success of the proposed rebellion that the English should be ready to rise against the Queen's Government; the whole scheme presupposed subdued revolt throughout her realm; the suggestion did but confirm what the friends of the Duke of Norfolk asserted. Hawkins fooled him to the top of his bent. Don Guerau promised that he would transmit the proposal to Spain and inform his confidant of the result. The ambassador wrote at once to King Philip's secretary, Cayas, and also to the Duke of Alva. He pointed out what a magnificent recruit to the cause of Spain in England such a man as Hawkins would be, and what influence he wielded among the seamen of all ranks. He confessed that Hawkins's character was shady, and that his reputation stank in the nostrils of good Spaniards. Hawkins had undeniably been a pirate. But that was not an uncommon profession among Englishmen in these latter days, and to tell the truth (the hit was a sly one) there was hardly any room for wonder, considering the ease with which Spain submitted to the process of plunder. He enlarged upon Hawkins's boldness and resolution, and upon his capability as a sea-captain and a soldier. He advised the King to accept the offer.

Alva seemed to see through it. He would not entertain the idea. King Philip also was suspicious. Hawkins of Plymouth? Ojo! When Hawkins went to the ambassador to get his answer, it was that Philip would not accept. Was there no hope at all? None, was the rejoinder — unless Hawkins himself would go to Madrid and state his case, or send some confidential person who could explain the matter and give assurances.

Hawkins in Madrid! The notion was preposterous. The victim of San Juan would not place his head in the hornet's nest again. But he might find a person who could go without danger; and he did find him m the shape of George Fitzwilliam. There is some doubt about Fitzwilliam's identity, but he is described as one of Hawkins's officers. The name may have been merely assumed for the occasion. Hawkins must have chosen him from among men upon whom he could place implicit reliance, and it is not improbable that he had some acquaintance or connection in Madrid, or the means of making it. The most likely thing is that he was known to the Duchess of Feria, an English lady who had been maid of honour to Queen Mary. The Duke of Feria was a member of Philip's Privy Council, and one of his most influential ministers. Hawkins charged Fitzwilliam with the mission to Spain, where he sought out the Ferias and opened the business to them. They procured him an audience of King Philip. Fitzwilliam then laid the whole of the plot before his Majesty. Philip could not get rid of his suspicions all at once; he was notoriously slow of thought and action, and his deliberation should have served him well in a question of this sort. The deputy declared that Hawkins was a true son of the Church, and could not endure the advance of heresy in England, that he had great grievances against Queen Elizabeth, and was passionately anxious to see her deposed and Mary Queen of Scots set in her place. In fact, he repeated with elaborations all the taradiddle that had taken in Don Guerau.

King Philip knew all about the privateer fleet of the West, which spoiled his ships and invaded his colonies, held his proclamations in contempt, and even made raids on his own coasts. It was this terrible fleet which Hawkins now offered to bring over to the side of Philip, Spain, and the true Church. It was unquestionably a tempting prospect. But Philip remained cautious. If he did not know what a line of Protestants since old William in Henry VIII.'s time Hawkins represented, he knew, at any rate, that he had not acted in the West Indies like a son of the true Church. Did Hawkins know the Duke of Norfolk? Had he any personal acquaintance with Mary Queen of Scots?

These questions were put to Fitzwilliam, who was obliged to answer them in the negative. But Hawkins, he said, was known to everybody by reputation; he stood on his reputation, his acquirements as a seaman, his influence in the fleet which he now offered to the King. Philip had a chance to accept the services of the finest sailor in the Western Seas, one of the most resolute fighting captains of the day, and a splendid fleet of fast ships which would be a terror to the enemies of Spain. All he was asked to do in return was to pay the wages of the seamen, to advance a little money for repairs which had been neglected by the niggling Elizabeth — and to release those few poor sailors for whom Hawkins had so great a compassion. King Philip could not but admit that it was a very good bargain indeed — if he could only trust "Achines!" Until he knew more of a certainty he would say nothing about it. Fitzwilliam should return to England, and tell the Admiral that if he would send a letter of recommendation from Mary Queen of Scots, his proposal would be entertained.

The sequel is amazing. The Ferias had none of the caution of leaden-footed Phihp. They believed in Hawkins, believed in the design, and believed in the triumphant overthrow of Elizabeth. They opened their hearts to Fitzwilliam on the subject of Queen Mary and the plot that was in progress in England; they gave him presents to take to the imprisoned Queen, and letters which would secure for him confidential treatment.

Hawkins's scheme thus began to unfold more astounding results than ever he could have dreamed of. All he wanted was the release of the survivors of San Juan. He was now in a fair way to get that, but he was also in possession of the inmost secrets of the deadliest enemies of the Queen he adored.

The acts upon which Hawkins now entered have been described as boldly Machiavellian. Machiavelli's conception of *vertu* was self-reliant ability; he warned his prince to acquire both the nature of the fox and that of the lion. In this enterprise Hawkins did display the characteristics of the fox, as at San Juan he had exhibited those of the lion. As his scheme unravelled itself in form so much more elaborate than he had expected, he came to the conclusion that he would not be justified in carrying it further on his own responsibility. The decision was wise. For a private person in the State to have conducted by himself an affair of this sort would have laid him open to grave suspicion. Hawkins had no hesitation in taking Cecil into his confidence at once, and urging him to obtain the consent of the Queen to the next step. Cecil could not refuse. His eyes were being opened every day to dangers which he had not fully apprehended. The letters from the Ferias to Queen Mary were quite sufficient to show the extreme urgency of the case. Cecil consented; the Queen consented; Hawkins went on with all the resources of the secret service of the day at his back.

Fitzwilliam went down to Sheffield and delivered his letters, when their contents had been fully mastered by the Queen's Minister. He tried hard to obtain speech with the Queen of Scots, but failed. This attempt to act without the assistance of the authorities served to show that Lord Shrewsbury, who was in charge of the royal prisoner, was incorruptible, sincere as the regard he entertained for her was known to be. Fitzwilliam communicated the result of the journey to his principal, and they agreed that Cecil should be asked to obtain for him means of access to the Queen, in order to receive her reply to the Feria letters and procure Hawkins's recommendation to King Philip. Hawkins wrote to Cecil (May 13th, 1572). His letter shows that his first consideration throughout was the fate of his poor sailors. Fie speaks of "the better obtaining of our men's liberty, which otherwise are not to be released" — that was unless the testimonial to Hawkins could be extracted from Queen Mary. "And if it shall seem good unto your Lordship, he" (Fitzwilliam) "may be recommended by such credit as to your Lordship shall seem best: for, unless she be first spoken with, and answer from her sent into Spain, the credit for the treasure cannot be obtained. If your Lordship think meet that Fitzwilliam shall be recommended to speak with her; if I may know by what sort your Lordship will appoint, there shall be all diligence for his despatch used. And hereof I most humbly pray your good Lordship's speedy resolution."

Cecil wasted no time. He did not confide in Shrewsbury, but in his letter of advice declared that friends of the man Fitzwilliam were prisoners in Spain. He had an idea that they might be liberated if the Queen would lend him her aid. Shrewsbury was to allow Fitzwilliam to see the Queen in private. Fitzwilliam was received with cordiality by the Queen of Scots, as any friend of the Duke and Duchess of Feria would have been. She agreed to write to Philip about Hawkins's men; she had no objection to do such a service for Englishmen in distress. Without placing too implicit a trust in Hawkins's ambassador, she did all that he required, and gave him letters to Philip and to the Duke and Duchess for delivery. Fitzwilliam went straight to Hawkins, who wrote to Cecil informing him of the continued success of the intrigue, and forwarding the letters.

"He hath also a book of gold (sent from her to the Duchess of Feria) with the Old Service in Latin; and in the end hath written this word with her own hand, *Absit nobis gloriari, nisi in cruce Domini nostri Jesu Cristi.* MARIE R.

"I would have brought your lordship the packet myself; but he would deliver it himself" (*i.e.,* to the Duchess'); "and requireth to have from me a speedy despatch for his departure into Spain: the which I would gladly your Lordship would determine.

"And if the course which I have begun shall be thought good by her Majesty, that I shall proceed; there is no doubt that three commodities will follow, that is:

"1. First, the practices of the enemies will be more and more discovered.

"2. There will be credit gotten hither for a good sum of money. [1]

"3. Thirdly, the same money, as the time shall bring forth cause, shall be employed to their own detriment: and what ships there shall be appointed (as they shall suppose to serve their turn), may do some notable exploit, to their great damage.

"I most humbly pray your Lordship to carry this matter so as Fitzwilliam may not have me in suspicion; and as speedy a determination for his despatch as conveniently may be."

This letter is dated the 7th of June. Froude does not seem to have examined it carefully; he attributes the list of "commodities" that would ensue from the scheme to Cecil and not to Hawkins.

Fitzwilliam had the ear of the Spanish ambassador, and told him what had been done. Don Guerau wrote to King Philip a letter with which Fitzwilliam was also entrusted. Having received his commission from Hawkins, he hastened to Madrid again. The scheme worked to a wonder. Fitzwilliam's arrival happened at the psychological moment. The Pope had blessed the conspiracy, and Ridolfi had come to the Spanish Court with the Papal sanction. The prospect was roseate, and everything travelled in harmony with Philip's desires. In these circumstances, as was to be expected, Queen Mary's letter was enough to disarm what remained of his suspicions. He accepted Hawkins's offer and his conditions. Fitzwilliam hastened back to Plymouth, where he arrived at the beginning of September. On the 4th of that month, Hawkins wrote from Kinterbury Street to Cecil in London:

"My very good Lord, — It may please your honour to be advertised that Fitzwilliam is returned from the Court of Spain; where his message was acceptably received both by the King himself, the Duke of Feria, and others of his Privy Council.

"His despatch and answer were with great expedition, and with great countenance and favour of the King.

"The Articles are sent to the Ambassador, with order also for money to be paid me by him, for the enterprise to proceed with all diligence.

"Their pretence is that my power should join with the Duke of Alva's power, which he doth secretly provide in Flanders, as well as with the power which cometh with the Duke of Medina out of Spain: and so altogether to invade this realm, and set up the Queen of Scots."

It may be observed in passing that the proposed strategy of this nebulous expedition was precisely the same up to a point as that adopted sixteen years later when the Armada sailed against England. There was this important difference — that Hawkins and the western fleet changed sides. The conspirator continues:

"They have practised with us for the burning of her Majesty's ships; therefore there would be some good care had of them: but not as it may appear that anything is discovered, as your Lordship's consideration can well provide."

It was foxy in the extreme; Hawkins did not want the Spanish suspicions aroused till the £40,000 which was to be provided for the fleet was paid over. He mentioned that Philip had entrusted to Fitzwilliam a ruby "of good price" for the Queen of Scots, together with letters, which Hawkins thought might be delivered to her; there was nothing of any importance in them. Philip's verbal message to the Queen was that he had now "none other care than to place her in her own." Hawkins suggested that it would be advisable to allow Fitzwilliam to have further access to the Queen of Scots to render thanks for the delivery of the prisoners, who were now at liberty. It must always be remembered that the exceptions to this were the cases of those men already in the hands of the Inquisition; the Holy Office did not release its clutch upon them, as we have seen from the narrative of Job Hortop. This, Hawkins suggested, would provide a colourable excuse for his Lordship to confer with Fitzwilliam more largely.

He sent to Cecil a copy of the pardon he had himself received from the King of Spain, "in the very order and manner I have it." Further pardons of an even more generous and comprehensive character were preferred to be presented to him by the Dukes of Alva and Medina, although, as he said, this was large enough, and accompanied by great titles and honours from the King — "from which may God deliver me!" John Hawkins as a Spanish grandee was a comic fiction' of Philip's imagination. Copies of letters from the Ferias, Duke and Duchess and their son, welcoming this portentous recruit to the good cause, were handed on to Cecil by Hawkins. "Their practices be very mischievous," he piously observed; "and they be never idle, but God, I hope, will confound them, and turn their devices upon their own necks." He wound up by announcing that Fitzwilliam was on the way to London, and that he would presently follow himself and wait upon the Queen.

In the sequel, Norfolk was beheaded, and there were some hangings. The chance of anything in the nature of a serious plot for some considerable time was very slight, for the Duke of Alva, reverting to his original view about Hawkins with a sense of disgust at his aberration, immediately washed his hands of the English Catholics and all their works. The sky was thus cleared by the bomb which Hawkins had devised and exploded, although he had no conception at first of its deadly nature. We shall not be wrong in assuming that his chief satisfaction was the liberation of his poor sailors, now on their way home, each with ten of Philip's dollars in his pocket.

The exact details of his pretended scheme are interesting. He was to take over sixteen ships and 1,600 men. He stipulated for two months' pay in advance, and the amount was actually made over by the Spanish ambassador, and by Hawkins handed to the Queen, who used it in works of defence; it was even a neater instance of turning Philip's guns on himself than the leading case of the Genoese ducats. The agreement is preserved among the Spanish archives. It was signed and sealed at Madrid on August 10th, 1571, between the Duke of Feria, representing King Philip, and George Fitzwilliam, representing John Hawkins. It provided that the sixteen ships should be armed with 420 guns, and the monthly pay was to be 16,987 ducats.

When particulars of the discovery of the Ridolfi plot began to leak out, there were, of course, some suspicions about Hawkins. It was inevitable. They were never entertained for a moment by those who knew that "a more devoted and loyal subject never lived." But some people were taken in by the pretence, and the doubts have persisted. Dr. Lingard was deceived, and quoted the agreement above-mentioned as proof that Hawkins had consented to betray his country for a Spanish bribe! Lingard says: "The secret was carefully kept, but did not elude suspicion. Hawkins was summoned and examined by order of the Council. Their lordships were, or pretended to be, satisfied, and he was engaged in the Queen's service." The letters cited show the injustice and folly of such a charge.

This is an episode to which it is no more useful to apply the ethics of the present day than to apply them to the slaving expeditions. The whole of Europe was mined and counter-mined with plots, and it was no discredit to a plain English seaman that he devised a scheme whereby none was injured and the life of his Queen and the liberties of his country were, very probably, saved. It is a more highly romantic story than the pages of most fiction contain, and it has the virtue of being perfectly true.

[1] It will be remembered that Hawkins stipulated for an advance for the payment of his crews and the equipment of his ships.

Chapter XIII - The Favour of the Queen

Whatever the world thought about Hawkins's part in the Feria affair, Queen Elizabeth placed the question of her own belief beyond all shade of doubt. He was her loyal servitor, the protector of her Crown and person. He was never a courtier, even in the same sense as Drake; but his affection for the Queen was deep, and it coincided as a spring of action with his inborn patriotism and his enthusiasm for the Protestant cause. And while Queen Elizabeth thought highly of him, the majority of his countrymen also held him in esteem. They all loved a bold sailor; Hawkins's boldness, courage, and seaman's capacity were recognised and appreciated everywhere. In that day you could not make a national hero by telegraph overnight, but as fast as fame could run it spread his popularity. His own narrative of the Third Voyage had been circulated widely throughout the country, and the details of the adventure of San Juan were treasured by every hero-worshipper of an adventure-loving age.

Even while the Feria design was being worked out, Count Ludovici, through the agency of Sir Francis Walsingham, was begging Queen Elizabeth to give Hawkins licence to serve him "underhand" against the Spanish power in Flanders, and declaring that not a Spaniard could land there while Hawkins kept the seas. His reputation as an admiral of ships and a captain of men was not confined to England. Elizabeth, however, was in no mind just then for the prosecution of privy warfare in Europe. The discovery of the Ridolfi plot and the defeat of the machinations of the Duke of Norfolk eased the situation at home. Elizabeth relied on her favourite weapon, the tongues of ambassadors, even, as in the Armada struggle thereafter, she kept her Navy short of gunpowder and depended on words instead. She affected to listen to the complaints of Spanish merchants about the depredations committed by the privateer fleet. The Dutch Admiral, de la Marck, was ostentatiously ordered to leave the Downs and Dover Roads, which for so long a time had been his rendezvous and headquarters. Ostentatiously — yes; but de la Marck knew that the ostentation was meant for the Spanish ambassador in London, through whose eyes King Philip saw what was passing in England, rather than for himself. He stayed six weeks at Dover after he had received the royal command, and then suddenly put to sea.

By some curious coincidence, he weighed out of Dover Roads just at the moment when a large Spanish convoy was approaching the Straits. He captured two of the biggest ships and chased the others till he harried them up the North Sea. England was no longer, nominally, hospitable to him; he must have a home and habitation somewhere; a few days later, watchers at Brille saw his topsails rising out of the sea. They saw him come into the roadstead with all his fleet; they saw him send ashore a messenger. The messenger announced that de la Marck demanded, in the name of the Prince of Orange, the surrender of the town. The inhabitants of Brille could imagine nothing more to their taste; they were sullenly acquiescent in the Spanish domination because the Duke of Alva had a garrison there. The garrison was no match for de la Marck's force; the thing was easy and bloodless. Within a very short time Brille was a strong citadel of Protestantism. Its example was infectious. The other coast towns of the Netherlands rose, overwhelmed the alien garrisons, and dragged down the holy banners of Spain. The Duke of Alva might tear his beard as he pleased. The seed that sprang up into a great Dutch Republic had been sown.

But Hawkins had no part in this; Elizabeth thought he had inflicted sufficient pin-pricks upon her brother-in-law for the time being, and wanted him for other business. He was again elected member for Plymouth in 1572, and the same year had a share in the operations for the relief of Rochelle. The story of this transaction is not preserved in any great detail, but the skeleton of it is interesting. It first crops up in a letter from Sir Thomas Smith to Cecil (January 8th, 1572). This was the Thomas Smith of *De Republica Anglorum* fame, who was in attendance upon the Queen at Hampton Court, through whom she sent her desires to Cecil in London. Hawkins had apparently suggested some scheme by which the Huguenots at Rochelle might be assisted, for Smith mentions that he had shown Hawkins's letter to the Queen. The Comte Montgomerie and Vidame were at court, and they were requesting the Queen to send Hawkins or another captain, under some pretence that might easily be invented, to Rochelle with supplies of gunpowder to replenish the magazines of its defenders. The only pretence that suggested itself to them was that which Hawkins himself had adopted at divers times in the West Indies: they recommended that he should pop up at Rochelle as from nowhere in particular, "driven thither by tempest or contrary winds."

There was nobody living better able to harness the elements to his purposes; but Elizabeth was doubtful. She was at peace with the King of France; it was notorious that the Prince of Conde's commission ran in a great many ships of the Plymouth fleet, for the French ambassador had only recently been complaining about it, and urging the Queen to give no countenance to this surreptitious assistance of the rebellious subjects of his master. Nevertheless, the Queen believed it necessary for the maintenance of the Protestant cause in Europe, on which the safety of her throne depended, that Rochelle should not fall to the besieging army; and at her request Sir Thomas Smith begged Cecil to "think of it, and devise how it might be done."

This was work of a sort for which Cecil had no liking; he detested these intrigues. But the events of the last two or three years had alarmed him; he did "think of it," and he devised how it might be done. Hawkins was the instrument he chose. It was a task after his very heart, and withal the easiest he had set his hands to. The last we hear of it is in a letter from Charles IX. of France to La Motte Fénelon (23rd February, 1573) making plaint that "M. Haquin" had joined with certain of his rebels near the Isle of Wight, with twelve or thirteen ships, had carried munitions and stores from England to La Rochelle, and had captured several French vessels. The taking of the French ships was not in the contract, but the Catholic *bâtiment* on the sea, with Catholic property on board, was fair game for a combined squadron of English and Huguenot privateers, and to have allowed it to go unransacked would have been to neglect the bounties of Providence. At La Rochelle in 1571 had been held the Synod of the Protestant Churches of France, under the presidency of Beza, to draw up a confession of faith. It was the stronghold, the one tower, of Protestantism on the Continent, and Hawkins's munitions, without doubt, helped it to withstand successfully the terrible siege in which the armies of the Catholic King lost 20,000 men, and then failed to reduce the place.

In this year of 1573, John Hawkins began his great career as administrator of the British Navy. It was a post to which he was called with universal approval. All his qualities recommended him for it — his sound judgment, his vast experience of the sea and sea fighting, of ships and ship-building, of seamen and their management, his business instincts, and his tremendous, indomitable energy and capacity for work. If Hawkins had known all the trouble and misery that this appointment was to involve for him he would never have accepted it. That would have been a great loss to the nation and its Navy, for the results he achieved by way of naval improvements and dockyard administration were magnificent. England had solid reason to be thankful that the tribulations which the future held were concealed from Hawkins in 1573.

It will be more convenient to deal with his official life in a separate chapter; one or two incidents that stand out in this time of transition from the character of sea-rover and adventurer to that of statesman may be fitly mentioned here.

Like her great father, Elizabeth admired a strong man. Hawkins had endeared himself to her, not only by the enterprise of voyages which had returned a handsome profit on her private outlay, not only by his vindication of the character of the fighting Englishman at San Juan, not only by his terrorisation of her enemies upon the sea. She realised the terrible danger she had just escaped, and knew that but for the scheme of guile which Hawkins had concocted for the release of his poor sailors, she might have lived only long enough to see her foes triumphant and a usurper in her place. Therefore when, in 1573, an attempt was made upon the life of Hawkins, her rage knew no measure. The Admiral was on his way to Court when he was attacked by a man who mistook him for Sir Christopher Hatton, a notorious member of the Catholic party. The assailant was Peter Burchet, a member of the Inner Temple, a fanatical Papist-hater, who would have killed Hatton like a dog if he had been lucky, and deemed the murder merit. Hawkins got out of the affair with one dangerous stab. After the first blow, he defended himself vigorously, overcame and seized Biurchet, and handed him over to justice. There was some peril that Hawkins's wound would prove fatal, and the Queen was so maddened by the possibility that she wanted to have Burchet tried by martial law, and strung up by the neck immediately without benefit of clergy. Essex persuaded her of the inadvisibility and illegality of such summary measures. Burchet was committed to the Tower. He struck his keeper over the head with a billet and killed him — and was hanged for that murder.

Sir Thomas Smith thus refers to the matter in a letter to Cecil: —

"Her Majestic taketh heavily the hurting of Hawkyns, and sent her own surgeons to hym, and Mr. Gorges to visite and comforte hym. It will sone appeare whether he can escape or no. Neither her Majestie, nor allmost any one here, can thynke otherwyse but that there is some couspiracie for that murder, and that Burchet is not indeede mad. It is said here that divers tymes, both by wordes and writings, Mr. Haddon hath bene admonished to take hede to hymself; for his life was laide in waite for. Mr. Garret told me that he had bene with one or two gentlemen that came out of the west countrey to London with Burchet, who declareth that he had many phantasticall speeches and doings whereby they might perceive that he was not well in his witts all the whole journey hitherwards."

One little story (the date is 1577) may be told, too, in order that it may not interrupt the narrative of Hawkins's career in the capacity of Elizabeth's Board of Admiralty. To him has been ascribed by some writers, though with nothing like sufficient evidence, the authorship of a strange anonymous letter received by Queen Elizabeth. Many a sounding blow had been struck at the sea-power of Spain during the last twenty years, but that power had not been crippled. The impression had become general that a crucial moment was approaching — as indeed it was — when the English and the Spanish nations would have to fight out in the open this vital question of the command of the sea. It was this conviction that originated the proposal now made to the Queen: a short way with Papists. It sounds cruel, bloodthirsty, barbaric at this distance of time; reading it, if one would see into the mind of the writer, he must bear in mind the *auto-de-fé,* and the torture chambers of the Inquisition, and the horrors of the Spanish galleys. Froude, who tells us that he found the letter in the Record Office, does not attempt to give its author a name. It was written in a bold round hand by "some inspired old sea-dog." This was certainly a time when the sea-dogs were inspired. Drake was about to set out for the great voyage of circumnavigation; he sailed in the following November, and returned three years later with his ships ballasted with Spanish treasure. But raid Spanish ships and Spanish colonies as they might, capture and destroy as they might, the privateers did not make any great impression on the vast bulk of Spain's sea-power. It was to strike a terrible blow at the very heart of that power that the author of the letter proposed.

He wanted the Queen to provide ships enough — five would do if they were well armed — for an expedition to the banks of Newfoundland, where the Spanish sailors were trained in seamanship, and every winter there was a great assemblage of merchant shipping belonging to Spain and other Catholic nations. He would, with his squadron, if Elizabeth would give him private letters of mark, take that shipping. "The best I will bring away, and I will burn the rest. Count us afterwards as pirates if you will; but I shall ruin their sea forces; for they depend on their fishermen for their navies. It may be objected that this will be against our league; but I hold it as lawful in Christian policy to prevent a mischief betimes as to revenge it too late...I will do it if you will allow me; only you must resolve, and not delay or dally. The wings of man's life are plumed with the feathers of death." God himself, the inspired sea-dog declared in a burst of elevation, was a party to the quarrel, and the malicious enemies of Queen Elizabeth were the enemies of God. It was, in his view, not a cold-blooded massacre, but a pious emprise to put an end to 20,000 Catholic seamen, and cause the galleons of Spain to rot in the harbour of Cadiz. But such a deed would have shocked the world, even in that era of blood, and the offer was not accepted.

The authorship of the proposal will probably remain a historical problem. Hawkins was not the man; he was not given to philosophising. Drake never accomplished a sentence like this: "The wings of man's life are plumed with the feathers of death," though he knew the truth of it in practice. Besides, Drake at the time was intent on other business. The best guess seems to be that of Mr. Worth — Sir Humphry Gilbert. Gilbert did moralise, and he was possessed of deep religious sentiment. To him we are indebted for the poetic aphorism, "Heaven is as near by water as by land." There we must leave it as a documentary curiosity, a sign of the times, a portent of the great cataclysm slowly and surely drawing near.

Chapter XIV - Elizabeth's Board of Admiralty

By the year 1573, Hawkins had been recognised as the greatest sailor of his time, as well as one of the ablest, astutest and most valiant of its men. In that year he was appointed Comptroller of the Navy, and Treasurer of the Queen's Majesty's Marine Causes, in succession to his father-in-law, Benjamin Gonson. He held office till after the Armada, and left his indelible mark upon the Navy as reformer, administrator, and inventor. Mr. Julian Corbett [1] has pointed out that when Elizabeth came to the throne, the Navy had vastly declined from the state of efficiency to which it had been brought in the reign of Henry VIII., when old William Hawkins commanded the *Great Galley.* During the early part of Elizabeth's *régime,* it remained inefficient: the work of England on the seas was being done by the privateers under such men as the Hawkinses. Compared with the Navy of Spain, that of England was contemptible.

"England," says Mr. Corbett, "was a first-rate naval Power before ever she (*i.e.* Elizabeth) came to the throne, and, after the scare which had followed the loss of Calais had worn itself out, the first part of her reign did little to increase the prestige she was heir to. Of her father's splendid Navy she had inherited little more than the ruin. Yet it must not be assumed that the naval policy which the first Tudors had inaugurated had been lost sight of by either of her predecessors."

The last remark is true enough: we have seen how politeness was exacted even from King Philip. But the fact stands that when Elizabeth had reigned ten years her fleet consisted of twelve fighting ships compared with the fifty or sixty that her father had been able to place in commission.

The approach of the conflict with Spain — it was felt it was in the air — rendered necessary naval organisation on a much larger and more complete scale. When the Queen and her Ministers cast about for a man to do this work, they could find no peer of John Hawkins. He was chosen because he was, without room for question, the fittest person in all the realm. The years he spent thereafter at the head of the Navy were years of terrible, grinding slavery for him, years of incessant devotion to the most exacting drudgery. He endured all like the stubborn Englishman he was. In his two offices of Comptroller and Treasurer, he found combined nearly the whole of the executive work now done by the Board of Admiralty. He had to keep the accounts of the fleet and all naval establishments — a difficult and delicate business indeed with such a mistress as Elizabeth. He had to manage and maintain the whole naval force of the nation. Were an expedition of any sort planned? — upon Hawkins fell the task of estimating the cost and making the arrangements. It was for him to keep the naval stores in good order. It was his duty to superintend the building of ships, and to see that the crews were provided and paid. Were harbour works projected? — it was for Hawkins to report on them.

It was an appalling task, a prodigious accumulation of all sorts of mental labour; it was too much for any one man, and it proved too much for Hawkins. He was not a demi-god; he had no supernatural aids; he was merely a hard, straight-ahead worker, with all the finest and strongest characteristics of his race highly developed. As well as one man could discharge this labour of Hercules, he did it. He spent himself in the service of the Navy in a heroic spirit of self-sacrifice that it cannot be easy to parallel.

He shared the duties of the Treasurership with Gonson for a year or two, till the death of the old man. Then the whole work of both posts fell upon him. His office was at Deptford; during these years his residence alternated between a house in St. Dunstan's-in-the-East and the family house at Plymouth. His supreme position was one in which a dishonest man, or a man with little of the finer scruple, might have piled up for himself a large fortune. John Hawkins did not make a penny out of it beyond his salary; on the contrary, he often had to advance money from his own purse for naval charges, and encountered great difficulty in the attempt to get it refunded. He was accused at various times of plundering the Exchequer; but these charges were proved baseless. It was Elizabeth's way to starve the Service, and to depend upon the Titanic labours of her devoted servants to supply what she left lacking in material provision for the defence of the country. She wanted the Navy improved and increased; it was very necessary that both improvement and enlargement should be secured; but at the same time she wanted the expenses reduced.

The unwelcome work of detecting and checking abuses and preventing the leakage of money wherever leakage could be found devolved upon Hawkins. He did it, with Spartan severity; and naturally he made a great many enemies in the process. Thus, at Chatham, he found himself in conflict with everybody in official position. People whom he displaced from sinecures became his bitter foes. People who were living on the proceeds of peculation, and suddenly found the source of their ill-gotten supplies closed up, were envenomed against him. The cleansing of the Augean stable at Chatham was the work of fifteen months. He stuck to it manfully, and succeeded in" effecting an economy of £3,200. Meanwhile, not only did he maintain the previous status of work at Chatham, but he greatly increased its volume and improved its quality. The details are shown in his correspondence with the Judge of the Admiralty. He was charged with injustice and deceit; it meant that he had discovered abuses and quashed them.

Throughout this rummaging into all the holes and corners of a neglected administration, Hawkins was no respecter of persons. He served high and low alike. From Sir William Winter to master-shipwright Baker, from Pett, the great ship-builder, to the humblest clerk or apprentice; if he found anything suspicious in their dealings, or anything fishy in their accounts, he called them to task for it. Winter was enraged. He made some of the most serious of all the false charges laid against Hawkins. He said: "When he was hurt, in the Strand" (referring to the attempt on his life by Burchet) "and made his will, he was not able to give £500. All that he is now worth hath been drawn by deceit from her Majesty." It was a manifest lie, for Hawkins was a rich man, and owned much property and great interests in shipping and trade at Plymouth. Happily, the persons most concerned, the Queen and her Ministers, paid no attention to the slanders so industriously propagated. He retained their confidence in the fullest degree.

Yet all these things made Hawkins's official life anything but a siesta on a bed of roses, and things did not improve as the great test of his administration grew near. Reference has been made to his foresight. It was never more conspicuously displayed than in these troubled years. All the while he was struggling with the difficulties created by the miserly mind of the Queen, and the corruption at Chatham and Deptford, he looked forward. The great day of England's trial loomed before his imagination and drew him to yet more strenuous effort. He had his eyes upon the sea and the sea-fighting that presently should be. No man in England had a truer conception of the reality of the political situation in Europe during the decade that followed the death of Gonson. He realised that the essence of the problem was sea-power, and that if the sea-power of Spain could not be crushed, the liberties of England and its very national existence were threatened. And he worked away doggedly, foreseeing the day of Armageddon, and determined that so far as he was concerned England should arise at the dawn of that red day prepared for all its chances, a strong man armed. He ranged unceasingly from the top to the bottom of the naval service, making dockyard improvements, improvements in ships, improvements in the *personnel* of the fleet, improvements in the armament and the equipment of all the maritime forces. Now and here, as ever and everywhere, he was the apostle of Thorough. At a time when his enemies were very lively in the land — at a much later date, when he was approaching the end of his career and fitting out the last expedition that he ever took to sea — Sir Thomas Gorges wrote of him: "Sir John Hawkins is an excellent man in these things; he sees all things done orderly." And now, while he was creating the Navy that was to meet the Armada, John Hawkins saw "all things done orderly."

He worked so hard, so continuously, so indefatigably, that he seriously impaired his own health. He fought against illness as he would have fought against a Spaniard, and worked on. The chief places of rendezvous for the royal ships were the Thames, the Medway, and the Downs. Hawkins saw what an immense waste of time was incurred by the absence of proper accommodation for ships of war further down the Channel. The scene of most of the employments of the Queen's ships was the coast of the enemy, or the open sea, or the far distant Western Continent. He recommended the formation of bases for them at the Isle of Wight, Weymouth, Dartmouth, Plymouth, and Falmouth, which would save the time and the cost of getting right up round the Nore for re-equipment or repairs. His policy in this, as in so many other matters, foreshadowed the practice of after years. Great developments began to be made immediately at Portsmouth. The dockyard at Plymouth (Devonport) was commenced a century later. Portland is now an important naval base, and both Dartmouth and Falmouth are extensively used by the smaller craft of the Navy.

Turning his attention to the *matériel* of the fleet, he was responsible for many improvements in the design of ships, in which, of course, he had the assistance of Pett and other builders. Hawkins saw Spain as the enemy, and he had not gathered all his experience of fighting the galleons of Spain for nothing. He perceived the advantage of ships that were handy and fast, even if they were smaller than the Spanish masterpieces, and of guns of long range. The fashion of naval construction hitherto had made the British Navy look like an assemblage of Chinese junks. The ships had great upper works, huge elevations fore and aft, and they were clumsy to handle. Hawkins cut them down. The *Jesus of Lubek* had been a more weatherly vessel after he reduced her upper-works during the gale in the Gulf of Mexico. He lengthened their keels, and made their lines finer. He improved their rig to enable them to haul closer to the wind. He gave them every advantage in every point of sailing over the Spanish model that his experience could suggest and his inventive genius devise. He saw that their armament was the best that could be obtained and the most effectively disposed. He introduced into them all the improvements that the lessons of his sea-life had taught him and the record of the privateers sanctioned. The superior sailing qualities of the English ships and their superior gunning had a great deal to do with the defeat of the Armada of Philip. Hawkins was a versatile maritime inventor. He devised boarding nettings. He invented chain pumps and introduced them into the royal ships. In every detail of the shipwright's craft he was ever looking for something better and often finding it.

Then, as to the, men who sailed the ships and worked the guns: we have seen his sympathy for his "poor sailors." It extended impartially to all the men who were ever under his command or control in any way. He raised the pay of the seamen from six and eightpence to ten shillings a month: it would probably work out to about £4 of our money. This was a bold step to take with Elizabeth in her most haggling mood; but he knew what it meant, and he convinced his employers that he was right. It would bring into the service better men, he said; and the better the men the more economically the work would be done, for fewer men would be required to do it. He liked to have decent, respectable, God-fearing sailors in his ships — "such," he remarked, "as could make shift for themselves, and keep themselves clean — without vermin." In Hawkins's gospel, cleanliness was next to godliness; he knew the importance of a clean bill of health on shipboard. He would recruit the Navy in the spirit in which Cromwell, at a later day, recruited his regiment of Ironsides. He knew the value of men of resource, who would not, in a moment of difficulty when leaders were lacking, be nothing but a collection of helpless cattle.

In a word, Hawkins got the Navy into a condition in which it was fit to meet anything that could be met at sea. It would have been bigger and better if Elizabeth had realised more fully the ordeal through which it must pass; but so far as his financial limits would allow him, he made it a perfect machine. As Froude says, "when the moment of trial came, he sent her ships to sea in such a condition — hull, rigging, spars, and running rope — that they had no match in the world."

Drake's star was in the ascendant in 1581. He had returned from his great circumnavigation, and the *Golden Hind* had been brought round to Deptford. The fabulous treasure that he had captured from the Spaniards in the Pacific was laid up in the Jewel House of the Tower. Hawkins felt no jealousy of the successes of his young kinsman, whom he had introduced to the art of adventure and the science of plunder in the Spanish Seas. He joined in the applause that greeted the Dragon's exploits, and reverberated throughout the world when the Queen went in state to visit the ship at Deptford, dined on board with the hero of the hour, and knighted him for his gallant services.

Drake proposed later in the year that Hawkins should join him in a fresh adventure. But the Treasurer had worked so hard that a severe illness had laid him by the heels. "My sickness doth continually abide with me," he wrote, "and every second day I have a fit. If I look abroad in the air but one hour I can hardly recover it in six days with good order." Adventurers could not lack for any enterprise in which Drake was concerned, he thought; but his own ability and state were not equal to it. His financial burdens from the last adventure were very heavy; he had to decline the offer. He remained at his post, working as hard as ever after his recovery, and ever preparing against the great day of trial with Spain.

In the summer of 1584, when Drake's adventure of 1585 was being discussed and organised, Hawkins submitted a scheme to Cecil, the object of which was "strongly to annoy and offend the King of Spain, the mortal enemy of our religion and the present government of the realm of England." The black clouds were gathering thickly. Hawkins noted the sinister aspect of the heavens. He wanted to strike the first blow in the fight for the final supremacy of Protestantism or the Roman system in England. William the Silent, after his long, heroic maintenance of the unequal contest in the Netherlands, had gone to a martyr's grave, stricken at Delft by the hand of an assassin whom Philip had hired for the bloody deed at a cost of twenty-five thousand crowns. Philip and the Pope were plotting again as vigorously as ever against the excommunicated Elizabeth. Within a few months the danger had become so ominous that the Bond of Association was formed and joined by Englishmen, Catholics and Protestants alike, all over the kingdom, sworn to protect the Queen against attacks, to avenge her death if it should unhappily be encompassed by violence, and not to recognise Mary Queen of Scots as her successor. Elizabeth had been induced to lend a grudging assistance to the Dutch in their fight for liberty, and for the principle enunciated by William of Orange that no man should be molested in his religious belief, whatsoever it might be. English vessels were being seized and English seamen maltreated in Spanish harbours.

But even now the Queen would not admit that open, honest war was inevitable. Everybody in England could see it but herself. Hawkins wanted to weaken the power of Spain for evil when the day of wrath came. So, from Deptford on the 20th of July, he addressed his letter and enclosed his scheme to Cecil.

He modestly set forth the reasons that in ordinary circumstances would incline him towards a peaceful life his own comfort and his financial wellbeing. As a trader, John Hawkins might have achieved a huge fortune; had he been content to follow the more mediocre course of his brother William, as a burgess of Plymouth, a merchant in the mart, and a sailor in the easy ways of trade, he might have lived a happier life. But he considered "whereunto we are born, not for ourselves, but for the defence of the church of God, our prince, and our country" — a lofty ideal of civic conduct, which he endeavoured to follow all these years of tribulation, reaping a harvest of misfortune and chiding. This was the inspiration of his plan whereby the government "might, with good providence, prevent the conspiracies of our enemies." He affirmed — Hawkins, who had for years been wrestling with cupidity and niggard doles for the great service he represented — that he doubted nothing of "our ability in wealth, for I am persuaded that the substance of this realm is trebled in value since her Majesty's reign — God be glorified for it!" It was a shrewd hit, to be followed by a shrewder. England did not lack ships, provisions, powder, armour, and all the munitions of war; of what use were all these and all the wealth of England if they were not used when they were needed? With an almost prophetic vision of the criminal miserliness of Elizabeth when the Spanish ships were sailing by the very harbours of her land, he exclaimed:

"I read when Mahomet the Turk took that famous city of Constantinople, digging by the foundations and bottoms of the houses, he found such infinite treasure as the said Mahomet, condemning their wretchedness, wondered how this city would have been overcome or taken, if they had in time provided men of war and furniture for their defence, as they were very well able."

The parable was plain: If Elizabeth maintained the course on which she was set, if Philip of Spain should prove a Mahomet — as happily the monarch of the *pie de plomo* did not prove — he might very well dig in the ruins of London, and, finding it a city of infinite riches, wonder however he had the good fortune to set foot in it. Hawkins asked pardon for dealing with "matters so high," but begged Cecil to ponder on the notes he enclosed, and judge of them by his great wisdom and experience.

It was a subtle scheme. Thoroughly to understand it, the history of the last four years in Portugal must be briefly viewed. The brave, imprudent Dom Sebastian had been killed in battle with the Moors in Africa in 1578, and his successor, the Cardinal Henry, died in the midst of disputes about the succession to his crown in January, 1580. Philip of Spain had bought over the Portuguese Cortes to the support of his pretensions, and had silenced the Duke of Braganza by offering him Brazil with the title of King. He annexed the crown without serious opposition. Thus began "the sixty years' captivity" — the sixty years of Portuguese vassalage to Spain from 1580 to 1640.

But immediately the settlement was effected, a pretender to the Portuguese throne arose in the person of Antonio, Prior of Crato, illegitimate offspring of Louis, Duke of Beja, and therefore grandson of Dom Emmanuel the Fortunate. He set up his standard at Santarem, proclaimed himself King, entered Lisbon, and struck money there. But he found the country cold; it was sunk in luxury, and had no energy to resist the pretensions of Philip. Antonio could raise no effective party. Philip sent an army against him under the Duke of Alva, who defeated him at Alcantara; Antonio fled to France, and Philip was declared king without further opposition. The Prior of Crato continued to advance his claims, and endeavoured to enforce them with foreign assistance. In 1582, he attacked the Azores with a strong French fleet commanded by Philip Strozzi. The French were routed in a battle with our old friend de Baçan, whom we met at San Juan, and Antonio this time fled to England. Alva's expedition against him in 1581 was his last. The aged butcher was dragged by Philip out of his imprisonment in the castle of Uzeda — where he had been confined soon after his return from the Low Countries for his concern in certain offences of his son — in order to conduct this campaign. The brief war against the Portuguese pretender was conducted with Alva's usual ferocity: he seized a great quantity of treasure in Lisbon, and the city and its suburbs were sacked by his army, with the usual accompaniments. Two years later Alva died.

In 1584 Dom Antonio was enjoying the shelter of Elizabeth's protection in England, and it is to the unfortunate Prior of Crato — for every step he took was dogged by ill-luck — that Hawkins refers wherever he mentions "the King of Portugal" in the scheme submitted to Cecil. That scheme was an alliance of the supporters of Antonio with the privateers of the West of England,

and of Flushing, the Huguenots, and the Portuguese in the islands, in Guinea and Brazil, financed from England, to undertake an expedition against the sea-communication of Spain, and to raid its coasts. It was, in his opinion, "the best way to annoy the King of Spain without charge to her Majesty." Antonio was formally to declare war upon Philip, and to head the alliance. His letters patent were to run throughout the cosmopolitan fleet; he was to appoint a deputy who should give licence to privateers — "to such as upon their own charge would serve and annoy the King of Spain as they might by sea and land." Antonio, in return for legalising the operations, was to have five or ten per cent, of the booty, as might be agreed. Queen Elizabeth was to appoint an officer to register the privateers engaged in this service, who should give them permission to use "some port of the West Countrye" as their headquarters, where they might lay up their ships, repair, victual, and sell their spoils; out of which transactions the Queen was to receive five or ten per cent. The privateers of whatever nation would only be allowed to take part in the glorious enterprise on condition that they engaged not to offend any other person but that person against whom King Antonio was warring; they were not to disgorge their captures anywhere but in the port agreed upon, where would be commissioners to examine each case, and to restore any goods taken from nations with whom the King of Portugal was at peace. There was to be martial law for all who committed piracy.

If these conditions were granted, Hawkins said, and men were allowed to enjoy what they lawfully took while engaged in this service, the best owners and merchant adventurers of London would join in, and the gentlemen of the West country would not be backward. He reckoned that it would be an easy matter to induce the Portuguese oversea to revolt continually, and make things hot for Philip in his new colonies, and the fisheries would afford an easy prey:

"The islands will be sacked, their forts defaced, and their brass ordnance brought away. Our own people as gunners (whereof we have few) would be made expert, and grow in number; our idle men would grow to be good men of war both by land and sea.

"The coast of Spain and Portugal in all places would be so annoyed as to keep continual armies there would be no possibility; for that of my knowledge it is trouble more tedious and chargeable to prepare shipping and men in those parts than it is with us."

He added that it might be advisable to work Sir Francis Drake's coming expedition in connection with this; if Drake went under the commission of Dom Antonio, anything that he might do would be "lawful," and the arrangement might be kept secret till they were ready to sail. Such a constellation of freebooters surely never shone in the imagination of any other man. If it had been got together and started upon the work that Hawkins proposed, no Spanish keel could have lived upon the seas. And yet, he pointed out, the King of Spain would be unable to make it a cause of war, because ostensibly England would not be involved. On the other hand. King Philip would probably be compelled to entreat her Majesty to forbid her subjects to continue in the enterprise, and to withdraw from those who remained in it the protection of her ports. But, Hawkins left it to be inferred, the damage would have been done; "there will be such scarcity in Spain, and his coast so annoyed, as Spain never endured so great smart. The reason is that the greatest traffics of all Philip's dominions must pass to and fro by the seas, which will hardly escape intercepting."

Very hardly indeed. But Elizabeth was not in the mood to risk such aggression; she contented herself with giving Drake *carte blanche,* and he sailed in 1585 for the great expedition to the West Indies, while Hawkins's still greater plan was shelved.

[1] "Drake and the Tudor Navy."

Chapter XV - An Admiralty Memorandum

Family traditions associating the Hawkins name with the sea service were unbroken from the time of old Master William Hawkins, born at the end of the fifteenth century, to his great-great-grandson, John, who was at sea in 1627 when he inherited the family estates. The immediate succession to the maritime glory of Sir John Hawkins was held by his only child Richard, the boy whom we have seen in the house in Kinterbury Street, listening to the narratives of his father's adventures on the Spanish Main. He was pledged to the sea ere even he was born, it may be said; and during the years of his father's absence in the West, his tutelage was spent under his uncle, William. The training he had — first in boat-sailing in the purlieus of the Cattewater, then in coasting trips, or brief voyages to the neighbouring continental ports — made him an admirable seaman before he was out of his teens. For his day and his surroundings, he was a youth of culture and wide reading, and his amiability and courtliness became a proverb in after years. The pride and affection with which John Hawkins beheld the boy grow to a stripling and the stripling to a man, learned as himself in all the sciences and arts that might assist the making of a perfect sailor, brave as himself, patriotic as himself, and withal far more polished, were what may be imagined in a rather taciturn man of strong feelings. Richard was twenty-two when, in 1582, his father gave consent for his first long voyage. He set out under the generalship of his uncle for a trading expedition to the West Indies, having command of one of the ships, and in that trip displayed the qualities that were afterwards to make him famous under the name of "the complete seaman."

John Hawkins's scheme for an amalgamation of the Protestant privateers under the flag of Dom Antonio having been rejected, he had no compunction about allowing his son to accompany Drake and Frobisher in the expedition of 1585-6. Richard Hawkins was in command of the *Duck,* one of the twenty-five ships of Drake's fleet, and took part in the conquest of San Jago, San Domingo, Cartagena, and San Augustin — an excellent schooling for the role he was to play in the Armada fight, and in his subsequent encounters with the Spaniards in the Pacific.

Hawkins, meanwhile, continued to make ready for the war with Spain, and to urge upon the Queen and her Ministers the importance of consistent naval policy, if they could show consistency in nothing else. He submitted a scheme for the future administration of the Navy by commissioners, suggested by his own hapless experience in his dual office. He kept the statistics of ships and their contents constantly up to date, and again in 1586 had been working so laboriously that he brought on another severe illness. His enemies the idlers and non-efficients were still busy; he defended his fidelity stoutly in letters to Cecil, and justified every step he had taken and every penny he had spent.

Drake's fleet returned from its triumphant raid upon the Spanish colonies in July, 1586, and Richard Hawkins sailed his galiot, the *Duck,* into Plymouth Sound with the rest of them. They had taken 200 brass cannon and 40 pieces of iron; they had £60,000 of prize money — not so much as had been expected, but still, enough to reward their crews and give the adventurers something. They had lost 750 men through the yellow fever; but they had inflicted many a telling blow on Philip, and had compelled the Catholic king and his ally the Pope to admit that the expedition against heretical England which had been discussed in secret, and was now being prepared, would be a very serious business.

John Hawkins had long realised what Elizabeth and her advisers failed to realise, that there must come a time — and that it was not far off— when all this patchwork of compromise would split into ribands, and the irresistible forces that were making for a contest at death-grips between the two systems they represented would break loose, run amok, and create havoc that would startle the whole world. Drake's expedition of 1585 — auspiciously commenced with a raid upon Vigo under Philip's very nose — brought matters to a crisis. Philip of the leaden foot had not previously moved in earnest. He was now impelled to action by pinpricks from every side. The Pope urged him on; his own Admirals urged him on. The Pope represented the danger and disgrace of allowing these piratical heretics to wreak their will upon his coasts and his colonies. The Admirals talked of the honour of Spain. Philip had hoped to gain his end by intrigue, and intrigue had broken down — year after year the hopes based upon the perfidy of Elizabeth's internecine enemies had proved the rottenest reeds. It was true that the Prince of Parma, who had succeeded Alva in the Low Countries, was apparently gaining ground and gradually Bringing the heretic Dutchman under his iron heel. But so far as England was concerned, the holy cause was making headway backwards. The plots against the life of Elizabeth were recognised, even by the better sort of Catholics at home, to be plots against the liberties of the nation: hence the Bond of Association. Craft and Conspiracy, all the underground schemes had utterly failed; Elizabeth despised them, walked unharmed amid Philip's armed spies, who were unnerved by her very boldness and contempt of personal danger; Philip must at last undertake the war of invasion which he hated.

He seemed to divine, if not its predestined failure, at least, the fact that he would gain no material benefits from it. Yet he could hold back no longer. Drake had settled that for him in the harbour of Vigo and in the islands of the West. Philip's trouble was now with the Pope. He saw that if events marched as his Holiness desired them to march, Spain and the power and dignity of its monarch would be in no sort advantaged. Rome would reap the benefits of a huge undertaking for which Spain would pay the price. Philip consequently asked for Peter's pence as well as for Peter's blessing upon his arms. He came to the verge of open quarrel with his Holiness on this point of the Papal contribution to the expenses of the enterprise. Sixtus V. did not trust Philip II. He would make no financial concessions, he said, till the army of Spain was landed upon the shores of England. He was not going to hand over a rich subvention for Philip to put it in his pocket first and choose how he should spend it afterwards. The mutual suspicion of the Head of the Church and the Catholic King was justified by events, and in any event must have been justified. If Philip had been successful, and had brought England to its knees, the result would have been merely to reduce the country to a condition of vassalage to Spain; Mary Queen of Scots bequeathed her rights in the English Crown to Philip, and when Sixtus learnt how the cat was to jump, he withdrew his support; when the Armada was disastrously defeated he made no attempt to conceal his satisfaction.

For the present, however, as matters stood between them, the Pope and the King were in agreement about the necessity of an attempt to reduce the heretical pretensions of England. Philip's personal desire would have been to hang back still; but other forces impelled him forward. He began to collect a fleet, deliberately, and to equip it, still more deliberately, with the idea that it should be in such overwhelming strength that unchallenged it might command the English seas. Then he might dictate what terms he pleased to the English people, suiting his own convenience rather than that of the Holy Father. The Invincible Armada was born.

This, I may repeat, John Hawkins had seen in prophetic vision — not in all details, but in all essentials. Even now, if Elizabeth and Cecil would have listened to him, he would have made the sailing of the Armada impossible. While yet the bruit of Drake's adventures was echoing through Europe, the busy mind of Hawkins was employed with the prospects of the coming strife. From on board the *Bonaventure* on the 1st of February, 1587, he submitted through Walsingham a project for scotching the Spanish snake. He had, he said, "of long time seen the malicious practices of the Papists, combined generally throughout Christendom to alter the government of this realm and bring it to Papistry, and consequently to servitude, poverty, and slavery," and he delivered his mind of a scheme for defeating the ends of the conspirators.

Anthony Babington's plot to murder the Queen had been discovered; the complicity in it of Mary Queen of Scots had been proved to as full demonstration as anything of the sort could be proved. The Scots queen had been removed to Fotheringhay Castle, her accomplices had been put to death, and she had faced her two days' trial. On the very day when Hawkins addressed his letter to Walsingham, Elizabeth — conquering her reluctance to shed the blood of her rivalsigned her death warrant. A few days later Mary died, having committed to Philip of Spain, almost with her last breath, the sacred task of the destruction of the heretic power of England.

Well might Hawkins animadvert upon the malicious "practices" of the Papists. As became good Christians, he declared, all Englishmen were exceedingly anxious to preserve peace, which was the best estate for all men. and he wished that by any means peace might be brought to pass. In his poor judgment, the right step was not taken, and the old sea-dog was not the man to cry peace when there was no peace. His "poor judgment" was confirmed by the verdict of history. The way in which Elizabeth meandered, even to the very moment when the Armada was upon her coasts, the way of compromise and confabulation, was not the way in which to handle a question of this kind.

"In my mind, our profit and best assurance is to seek our peace by a determined and resolute war!" Thus Hawkins — and a notable saying, surely — an aphorism drawn out of the deepest heart of man's long experience of a state of peace which was no peace, both at home and overseas. War, he said — open war, decisive war against the malign foes of England now plotting in the dark against its honour, its religion, and its well-being — would now be less costly, it would now more fully assure the safety of the nation, than the elaborate and artificial system of public negotiations and privateering which Elizabeth preferred. It would enable them to discern friends from enemies at home as well as abroad, and it would best allay the growing fears and suspicions of the whole community. There was need for such discernment. It was difficult to pierce the miasma that again overhung the land. There were Catholics in open opposition to the Protestant system and to Elizabeth's government; there were Catholics who sympathised in secret with the enemies of the queen, but would risk nothing openly to advance their ideal. The report which Father Parsons, the Jesuit leader, wrote for the eye of the Pope, dealing with the state of parties in England, is sufficient evidence of the spiritual and political turmoil that boiled under the smooth surface contrived by Elizabeth's complicated policy of compromise and half-measures. Already the advice of Parsons was being followed; the Armada was forming in the ports of Spain, the army of the Prince of Parma was being prepared for the crossing of the Channel.

As for the prosecution of the war which he recommended, Hawkins advised that it should not be carried into foreign countries, except when and where it might be absolutely necessary for strategical purposes; "for that breedeth great charge and no profit at all." He knew that England's strength was on the sea, and that, with the material she had for sea-fighting, she could hold her own. The measure of her success would be according to the administration of her sea-policy. He would blockade the coasts of Spain, harry the Spanish commerce, and terrorise the Spanish Navy. This work could be done with very little drain upon the resources of England: six of the best of the Queen's ships would suffice. And six of such ships as Hawkins had lately been building in the Thames could perhaps have done it. They should be victualed for some months, they should be accompanied by six smaller vessels to act as scouts — the little crowd of cruisers flitting round the battle fleet — they should haunt the coast of Spain and the islands, and be a sufficient force to account for any squadron, any convoy, that might pass to and from the Spanish harbours across its path. They would have to return to refit and repair: then six other good ships should take their place — "so should the seas be never unfurnished; but, as one company at the four months' end doth return, the other company should be always in that place."

The provision of this squadron, Hawkins pointed out, would not interfere with the efficiency of the home fleet, which would remain in strength enough to deal with any attempt that might be made at reprisals in English waters. He sent a note of the ships which, he suggested, might be detailed for this duty, and showed what force would then be left to guard the interests of England at home. "In open and lawful warfare," he concluded, in sonorous phrase, "God will help us, for we defend the chief cause, our religion — God's own cause. If we would leave our profession and turn to serve Baal (as God forbid, and rather to die a thousand deaths) we might have peace — but not with God."

Admiralty memoranda are not so couched in our day; but the Protestant religion was the ideal set high that led on the seamen of the sixteenth century to their most glorious achievements, and Hawkins meant every word he said. As usual, Elizabeth did not seize the opportunity; even yet she believed that open hostilities could be staved off. The Spanish fleet was fitting out in the Spanish estuaries; the Fiery Cross was being rushed through Catholic Europe to rouse men for the "enterprise of England"; but she would take no decisive step. Pin-pricks, singeing of beards, negotiation, compromise — these were her methods and her weapons still. She consented to another proposal of Drake's— to undertake an expedition furnished forth by the merchants of London, who provided the brilliant corsair-admiral with twenty-six vessels, to which Elizabeth added four ships of war and two pinnaces. The *Bonaventure,* from which Hawkins had dated his letter to Walsingham, was one of the four, and became Drake's flagship. So averse was Elizabeth from acting in the open that Drake had almost to sneak out of Plymouth Sound with his expedition, bound for Cadiz and the singeing of Philip's beard, for fear that the Queen should repent of her boldness. Indeed, she did send orders that he was to enter no Spanish port and injure no hair of a Spaniard's head: they arrived at Plymouth after he had sailed. The story of Cadiz needs no retelling here; one thing it proved — that if Hawkins's plan had been adopted, the Armada might never to this day have sailed from Spain.

Chapter XVI - The Armada

The Armada did sail from Spain. The day came when Elizabeth could temporise no longer, when guns took up the argument and spake to greater purpose than the lips of commissioners and the pens of diplomatists. The story of the great enterprise and its failure does not belong to the life of Hawkins, but to the history of Europe. It has been told often and eloquently on both sides. There is no intention of repeating it here, or of entering into any of its details save those in which John Hawkins was intimately concerned.

A small expedition of Thomas Candish to the West Indies, doing a great deal of damage, Drake's exploit at Cadiz, and Walsingham's successful interference with Philip's financial schemes at Genoa prevented the Spanish ambition from materialising in 1587, as had been intended. It was postponed till wet and stormy 1588, the thirtieth year of Queen Elizabeth's reign, the year which German astrologers had foretold was to be the "climacterical year" of the world. Whatever may be thought of that, 1588 was the dimacterical year of the life of John Hawkins, though he was still seven years off his grand climacteric in age. It probed the whole usefulness of his career. Had Hawkins been a hollow man, England's cause had collapsed. This was the test of all his achievements and all his energies — as an administrator, as a seaman, as a general. He was not found wanting.

His great care at the end of 1587 was the perfection of the Navy as an instrument of war. He was so earnest, dogged, sincere, unsparing of himself, that, without inquiry or investigation into the character of his work, that nearest possible approach to perfection at which he aimed might have been taken for granted. Inquiry and investigation were not spared, however; the examination into the condition of the fleet was conducted by Sir William Winter and William Holstock. At least one of these had no prejudice in his favour, as we have already noted in connection with the retrenchments at Chatham; but they reported without reserve that Hawkins's duties had been satisfactorily performed. Ere yet the Armada had sailed (in November) he made one more offer of personal service and individual action — to undertake with seventeen ships and pinnaces to prevent the landing of a foreign Power upon any of the western coasts of England. He was wanted for bigger things; for the moment he could not be spared from his administrative office; when it came to fighting, he was reserved for the command of the Navy as Vice-Admiral and for the task of supplying the professional defects — defects merely of inexperience — that underlay the magnificent qualities of the Commander-in chief, Lord Howard of Effingham. His present duty was to get the whole Navy of thirty-eight vessels in immediate condition for sea service at any emergency. Hawkins did not delay. In spite of cheeseparing, his preparations were so complete to the minutest detail that the command entailed no difficulty. In the Medway lay his finest contributions to the naval strength of England — five ships, four of them built according to his new design:

The Ark Royals 800 tons. This fine vessel became the flagship of Lord Howard, and the Lord High Admiral wrote of her to Cecil: "I praie your Lordship tell her Matie from me that her money was well geven for the Arke Rawlye, for I think her the odd ship in the worlde for all conditions, and truely I think there can no great ship make me change and go out of her."

The Victory, 800 tons. The Victory became the flagship of Hawkins as Vice-Admiral.

The Bear, 900 tons.

The Elizabeth Jonas, 900 tons.

The Triumph, 1,000 tons.

Of these, the Ark Royal was the only ship not of the new type. She preserved, though not in the most exaggerated fashion, the characteristics of the older class of ships of the line — high bulwarks and tall upperworks, fore and aft. In an engraving to be seen in the British Museum she is represented as a four-masted, square-rigged ship, which no doubt had all the qualities claimed for her by Howard, and was sea-worthy enough; but she had not the appearance of a very handy craft for rapid manoeuvring, and that was the principal advantage owned by her sisters. They, the other four, of equal and larger tonnage, had all Hawkins's improvements developed in their construction. Hawkins suffered the fate of all reformers and innovators in all time. His new ships were distrusted by the old school of seamen, and the usual adumbration of disaster was not wanting. So strongly was the feeling of distrust expressed that Elizabeth did not care to risk them at sea until they were absolutely required for active service, and they were never commissioned till 1588, though they were laid down several years before, and had long been completed. When they did go to sea they perfectly justified Hawkins; their performances bore out all his theories, and they were more useful than any other vessels in the fleet. They combined all the excellences to which allusion has been made above — fast sailing and facility of handling, and in their armament every improvement that Hawkins's long experience of sea-fighting had suggested.

Elizabeth continued to pare the cheese to the very last. Howard having been commanded to take the ships to sea (the order was given in December, 1587) "to defend the realm against the Spaniards," the next month it was made known that the fleet would be required for no more than six weeks, as the Queen hoped that a peace might yet be patched up. Crews for the thirty-eight ships had been obtained at the cost of immense pains to Hawkins and his subordinates, and at great expense to the State. There was a rumour that the Armada was about to be dissipated and Philip's scheme abandoned; Elizabeth dismissed half the sailors! Hawkins, the apostle of open and resolute "warre," was thrown into a state of mind that may be shared by any zealous officer who sees his best schemes running the risk of destruction through the folly of his employer. He declared (February, 1588): "We are wasting money, wasting strength, dishonouring and discrediting ourselves by our uncertain dallying."

Then, in another fortnight, the ships were ordered to sea again, and the harbours of England were scraped for men to fill them up. Bounties and allowances had to be given to tempt men to serve. Wasting money, indeed! The provisions for the fleet were cut down to the smallest possible limit. Meat was stopped; the crews were fed on fish, dried peas, and oil. Howard ultimately collected his fleet at Plymouth, but was allowed no stores from which to replenish it. Sometimes his men were without official rations for days together. This policy had its effect. The four new ships at Chatham could not be manned, and were delayed there for weeks. It was not until the Armada was just about to sail that they were put in commission. Then there was a great scurry for men and stores. Even so, only enough stores were contracted for to last till the end of June, and Philip's fleet was not in sight till three weeks after that.

Leaving a squadron under Seymour to aid the Dutch in watching the Duke of Parma and his flat-bottomed boats, Howard in the *Ark Royal* and Hawkins in the *Victory* went round to Plymouth to join the main body of the royal fleet and the privateer squadron under Drake there assembled.

The storm that hampered the Armada upon its first sailing in May, and compelled its return to port to refit, seemed at one time likely to be no godsend to England. False reports as to the nature of the impediments that Philip was meeting were spread; Elizabeth, thinking the Spanish fleet had been destroyed, or so seriously damaged that it could not possibly make the projected attack till the next year, again ordered reductions in the number of her ships in commission. Fortunately for the nation, Howard had better information, and refused to decrease his strength. Later on he had to use some strong language for the benefit of his royal mistress. Yet the policy of short commons was pursued. It is amazing that the loyalty of the commanders and the spirit of the men were not shaken by the extraordinary shilly-shallying, the niggling, narrow economies, the petulant nagging of the Queen. At the end of the first week in June the fleet had provisions for eighteen days. The material for re-victualling did not arrive at Plymouth till the 23rd; then there were provisions for a month only, and they were accompanied by a declaration that no more would be sent. Rank beer killed many men, and made more very ill. Howard procured wine and arrowroot for the sick. His difficult mistress called him sharply to account for this expenditure afterwards, and to avoid a disturbance he paid the money from his own pocket. The Lord High Admiral made the best of the wretched situation. He arranged that the month's rations should be made to last six weeks; but the quality of his temper may be seen in his note to the Queen on July 3rd: "For the love of Jesus

Christ, Madam, awake and see the villainous treasons round about you against your Majesty and realm."

All through the early part of July they waited for the approach of the Spaniards, either in harbour at Plymouth or cruising in the chops of the Channel, the fleet split into three divisions, spread out like a fan between Ushant and Scilly. Howard had the biggest squadron in the centre; Drake, with twenty ships and four or five pinnaces, saw that no Spaniard slipped up by the Isle of Ushant; while Hawkins, with a similar force, lay out on the right wing towards the Isles of Scilly. A fair north wind arriving, it was decided in a Council of the Admirals to sail down to the Spanish coast, with the object of crushing the Armada before it could reach English waters. They were forty leagues off Finisterre when news was brought to Howard that the Spanish fleet in Corunna and elsewhere was in a state by no means as crippled as had been reported. The wind shifted to the south, and his council thought it well to hurry back to the Channel before the Armada took advantage of the same breeze. They were home at Plymouth on the 12th July, and rode out there some very stormy weather, Howard and the big ships lying in the Sound, exposed to the south-wester, and the little ones running up the Cattewater for protection.

At home Hawkins found that his enemies in London were busy with his name. The *Hope,* a 600-ton vessel, commanded by Robert Cross, had sprung a small leak, and had gone into port to repair. This was enough for the crowd of people whom Hawkins had offended; they attacked his character as a naval official, and prognosticated darkly. "I have heard," wrote Howard to Walsingham from Plymouth on July 17th, "that there is in London some hard speeches against Mr. Hawkins because the *Hope* came in to mend a leak she had. Sir, I think there were never so many of the Prince's ships so long abroad and in such seas with such weather as these have had with so few leaks, and the greatest fault of the *Hope* came with ill grounding before our coming hither, and yet it is nothing to be spoken of; it was such a leak that I would have gone with it to Venice." It was a fine retort; Hawkins was well satisfied with a testimonial so thorough from the Lord High Admiral.

Two days after the letter was written the Spanish Armada sighted the English shores, and Captain Fleming, in his pinnace, came sailing into Plymouth with the news of its approach. Tradition — and there is no other basis for the story — says that when Fleming ran before the south wind across the Sound with his intelligence, the principal commanders of the fleet were all ashore, and that Fleming disturbed them at a game of bowls upon the Hoe. Drake, according to the legend pictorially represented by Mr. Seymour Lucas, insisted on completing the match, saying that there was plenty of time to finish the game first and beat the Spaniards after. It is a good Drake story, and deserves to be true. We must leave it at that. In any case, it is probable that the Admirals and many of the commanders were on shore. Hawkins was at home; his brother was Mayor of the town; he would have entertained his friends in Kinterbury Street, no doubt; William and John Hawkins had ships in the volunteer fleet, and his son Richard commanded the *Swallow,* a 300-ton ship of the Queen's Navy.

No time was lost before getting ready to meet the Spaniards. The English Admirals had some difficulty in working out of the harbour in face of the wind that was bringing the Armada up Channel with their sails full; but it was accomplished by the Saturday morning. By three in the afternoon they were all out in the offing, and Howard was manoeuvring to get the wind of the enemy. He succeeded completely. At nine o'clock on Sunday morning the whole Armada was seen westward of the Eddystone Reef, forming a great half-moon of stately ships, in comparison with which the English fleet looked puny. But this had the weather berth, it had the faster ships, the better guns, and the most daring seamen.

From on board the *Victory,* on the last day of the month, Hawkins wrote to Walsingham an account of the events of that crowded ten days — succinct, characteristic, making little mention of his own part in them. I carry on the story in Hawkins's own words, and fill in the ellipses afterwards.

"We met with this fleet somewhat to the Westward of Plymouth upon Sunday in the morning, being the 21st July, where we had some small fight with them in the afternoon. By the coming aboard one of the other of the Spaniards, a great ship, a Biscane, spent her foremast and bowsprit, which was lost by the fleet in the sea, and so taken up by Sir Francis Drake the next morning. [1] The same Sunday there was, by a fire chancing by a barrel of gunpowder, a great Biscane spoiled and abandoned, which my lord took up and sent away. [2]

"The Tuesday following, athwart of Portland, we had a sharp and long fight with them, wherein we spent a great part of our powder and shot, so as it was not thought good to deal with them any more till that was relieved.

"The Thursday following, by the occasion of the scattering of one of the great ships from the fleet which we hoped to have cut off, there grew a hot fray in which some store of powder was spent, and after that little done till we came near to Calais, where the fleet of Spain anchored and our fleet by them, and because they should not be in peace there to refresh their water or to have conference with the Duke of Parma's party, my lord admiral, with firing of ships, determined to remove them, — as he did, and put them to the seas, — in which broil the chief galleass spoiled her rudder, and so rowed ashore near the town of Calais, where she was possessed of our men, but so aground as she could not be brought away.

"That morning, being Monday, 29th July, we followed the Spaniards, and all that day had with them a long and great fight, wherein there was great valour shown generally of our company in that battle. There was spent very much of our powder and shot; and so the wind began to grow westerly a fresh gale, and the Spaniards put themselves somewhat to the Northward, where we follow and keep company with them. In this fight there was some hurt done among the Spaniards. A great ship of the galleons of Portugal spoiled her rudder, and so the fleet left her in the sea."

So wrote Hawkins while the wind had hardly blown away the powder-smoke, and the unhappy Medina Sidonia's fleet was racing away to the north, teased as far as the Firth of Forth by the English ships which buzzed behind him like a cloud of hornets. He proceeded to sum up the matter:

"Our ships, God be thanked, have received little hurt, and are of great force to accompany them, and of such advantage that, with some continuance at the seas, and sufficiently provided of shot and powder, we shall be able, with God's favour, to weaiy them out of the seas and confound them."

Like all other English seamen, Hawkins could not understand why with a force still so great, in spite of the damage that had been inflicted upon it, the Spanish Admiral turned tail and ran.

"As I gather, certainly there are among them so forcible and invincible ships which consist of those that follow, — viz: 9 galleons of Portugal of 800 tons apiece, saving two of them are but 400 tons apiece; 20 great Venetians, and argo-sies of the seas within the Strait (of Gibraltar) of 800 apiece; one ship of the Duke of Florence, of 800 tons; 20 great Biscanes, of 500 or 600 tons; 4 galleasses, whereof one is in France. There are 30 hulks and 30 other small ships, whereof little account is to be made. At their departing from Lisbon, being the 19th May, by our account they were victualed for six months. They stayed in the Groyne 28 days, and there refreshed their water. At their coming from Lisbon, they were taken with a flaw, and 14 hulks or thereabouts came near Ushant, and so re-turned with contrary winds to the Groyne, and there met. And else there was none other company upon our coast before the whole fleet arrived. And in their coming now, a little flaw took them 50 leagues from the coast of Spain, where one great ship was severed from them, and 4 galleys, which hitherto have not recovered their company.

"At their departing from Lisbon, the soldiers were 20,000, the mariners and others 8,000; so that in all they were 28,000 men. Their commission was to con-fer with the Prince of Parma (as I learned) and then proceed to the service that should be there concluded. And so the Duke to return into Spain with these ships and mariners, the soldiers and their furniture being left behind. Now this fleet is here and very forcible, and must be waited upon with all our force — which is little enough. There would (should) be an infinite quantity of powder and shot provided and continually sent aboard, without the which great hazard may grow to our country; for this is the greatest and strongest combination, to my under-standing, that ever was gathered in Christendom. Therefore, I wish it of all hands to be mightily and diligently looked unto and cared for.

"The men have been long unpaid, and need relief. I pray your lordship that the money that should have gone to Plymouth may now be sent to Dover.

"August now Cometh in, and this coast will now spend ground tackle, cordage, canvas and victual, all which would be sent to Dover in good plenty. With these things and God's blessing our Kingdom may be preserved, — which being ne-glected, great hazard may come. I write to your lordship [3] briefly and plainly: your wisdom and experience is great. But this is a matter far passing all that hath been seen in our time, or long before.

"And so, praying to God for a happy deliverance from the malicious and dangerous practice of our enemies, I humbly take my leave. From the sea, aboard the *Victory,* the last of July, 1588.

"The Spaniards take their course for Scotland. My lord doth follow them. I doubt not, with God's favour, but we shall impeach their landing. There must be order for victual and many powder and shot to be sent after us."

This, written "in haste and bad weather," as he informs us, was Hawkins's plain, sailor-like dispatch announcing the defeat of the Armada. His own part in the ten days' work was left for other pens to tell.

[1] This was the *Capitana,* commanded by Pedro de Waldez, and the mishap occurred in collision with the *Santa Catalina.* She had a large sum of money on board, and a number of jewelled swords, destined by Philip for the Catholic peers of England. Drake captured her after she had made a gallant fight, and took her into Dartmouth. The booty was the subject of an unedifying dispute between Drake and Frobisher.

[2] Oquendo's great galleon, which carried the Treasurer of the Fleet and 55,000 golden ducats. The disaster was attributed to the act of her Flemish gunner, and said to be a revenge for insults. It cost 200 lives. Howard took part of the money to pay his seamen, and was afterwards charged with peculation!

[3] As Hawkins explains to Walsingham in a postscript, this is a copy of a letter he is sending to Cecil, "whereby I shall not need to write to your honour. Help us with furniture, and with God's favour we shall confound their device."

Chapter XVII - The Fight with the Santa Anna

By no merit in the Queen and her Ministers was the Spanish Armada beaten off her shores — unless it were a merit and a contribution to victory to starve the sailors, worry the admirals, and keep the guns without powder. The perversity of Elizabeth's policy towards the fleet was simply wicked. The story of those stormy July days is an alternation of brilliant displays of strategy and courage with piteous appeals for provisions and ammunition. While the ships were within reach of Plymouth, William Hawkins sent out to them what he could. Thereafter the power of Howard was crippled, and the whole cause was more than once in danger because the Queen had not seen fit to spend the money that would have provided him with what he wanted. On the night after the first engagement, a courier was despatched to London with a message praying for a supply of ammunition. "Many of our great guns stood as cyphers and scarecrows," said Raleigh. After the fight off the Isle of Wight, Howard could not engage the Spaniards again until they were off Calais for lack of powder and ball. When the worst of it was over, and the Spaniards were flying, the English clung to their heels, though their men were in rags, with just sufficient food to keep them alive, and no means of firing their guns; they had, as Drake said, "to put on a brag, and go on as if we needed nothing."

It was well for England that the Spaniards were ignorant of the condition of her fleet, and that they were commanded by Medina Sidonia, rather than by such a man as the captured Dom Pedro de Valdez, or the fiery Oquendo. The situation is reflected in Hawkins's letter, written while the English were pursuing their beaten foe up the North Sea. Powder! Victuals! — with these things and God's blessing they might be able to carry the campaign to a successful issue. Elizabeth apparently thought the blessing of Providence alone was sufficient for their subsistence.

In the first action, off the Eddystone Reef, Hawkins, Drake, and Frobisher pointed up to windward so effectively with "their fast ships that they had no difficulty in keeping the weather of the Spanish line, and launching themselves persistently at the rearmost ships under Recalde. The surprise of the Spanish seamen (who were no mean mariners) at the manner in which the English vessels outpointed and outmaneuvered them, and at the range of their guns, has been the theme of many pens. The damage inflicted upon the helpless bodies of the great galleons was enormous. Keeping the weather berth, the Vice-Admiral and his companions reached again and again across the end of the line, giving them broadside after broadside, and quickly getting out of reach of their fire. When the English were within range, the Spanish guns were comparatively harmless because of their leeward position; as they heeled over to the merry south-wester, their cannonballs flew innocuous over the heads of their assailants. The fate of the *Capitana* and the *Santa Catalina* has been noted. Oquendo's "great Biscane" was battered into a hulk. Boats were sent from other Spanish ships to take off the men who remained on board after the explosion, but they had no time to remove the wounded, who were lying about among the corpses on her charred and blood-stained decks when the English took possession of the wreck. John Hawkins and Lord Thomas Howard put off in a cock-boat from the *Victory* the next morning, and went on board Oquendo's ship. Their examination revealed a terrible carnage, and the Lord High Admiral detached a small vessel to convey the ruins of the mighty galleon into Weymouth.

The hottest hour that Hawkins had was in the great fight off the Isle of Wight on the 25th. The weather had fallen calm. A large galleon of Portugal, the *Santa Anna,* had dropped astern of the rest of the Spanish fleet, and seemed to Hawkins likely to constitute a fair prize for a bold man. While the two fleets were becalmed, he managed to lay the *Victory* alongside the *Santa Anna,* and a great duel of the sea was fought between them, with the Spanish ships for spectators on the one side and the English on the other. To the Spaniards, the odds all seemed to be on their side; the galleon was bigger that Hawkins's flagship, and was full of sailors and soldiers; the daring Englishman appeared to be devoting himself to destruction. There was now no question of superior sailing and the advantage of the windward berth. In the flat calm, the sails of all the fleets hung limp and motionless. The only mobile

106

instruments of war upon the scene — or so it seemed till it was proved what the arms of the English oarsmen could do — were the galleasses that accompanied the Spanish fleet. It was therefore a desperate fight at close quarters, and the Spaniards had no doubt of the success of the *Santa Anna.*

They reckoned without their host; they reckoned without Hawkins's superior skill and heavier metal. De Baçan, who had fought with him at San Juan, would not have been so confident. Hawkins's guns fired the faster, and his men were in the higher spirits. The two ships pounded each other with their broadsides, and the rattle of the small arms was incessant, till they were wreathed and half hidden in powder-smoke, hanging heavy in the air and floating slowly over the oily sea. It had appeared quite an indecisive action till Hawkins got the vessels locked, and the gun-fire ceased while he led his men up the sides of the great galleon with their boarding weapons, and their fierce rush carried everything before them. The Spanish gunners were driven from their guns and forced back impotent. The English were on the soldiers before they could reload their pieces, so furious was the onslaught. In a few minutes it was all over. To avoid further slaughter, the Spanish captain surrendered; on his own quarterdeck, he delivered his sword to Hawkins, and the fighting ceased. Down to the deck dropped the banner of Spain; a little ball was run up to the main, and presently the English flag was broken out. The men of the *Victory* hailed it with loud huzzas, which were echoed back from the English fleets.

But the Spaniards were not content to allow so valuable a prize to fall to Achines without a further struggle. The fight was hardly over when three large galleys drew out from the main body of the fleet, and bore rapidly down, urged by their hundred sweeps, upon the pair that occupied the centre of this strange picture. It was likely to be awkward for Hawkins; the galleys were out of range of the English fleet, and, attacking him from three points at once, they were pouring metal into him and threatening to board him before anything could be done, Maneuvering was impossible; he had to be content with replying as the position of his guns would permit to the stings of the wasps humming around him. The English had no galleys; but they were to show that the fleet was not without strong-armed oarsmen, and its admiral not without ingenuity. Howard of Effingham had the longboats of his own ship, the *Ark Royal,* and others dropped into the water, and with great labour the flagship and the *Golden Lion,* commanded by Lord Thomas Howard, were towed down to the scene of conflict. Firing on the Spanish galleasses as soon as they got within range, they finally turned the tide in favour of Hawkins, and the great Portugal was left to her fate. A spirited attempt had been made to save her, but it had failed, and the three galleys, sorely battered, plied their long tiers of oars to get out of range.

Next day, Hawkins became Sir John Hawkins. Howard visited the *Victory* in state, and knighted the vice-admiral on his own quarter-deck. It was of old reckoned the highest honour that a man could receive to be knighted on the field of battle; the knighthoods which Howard sparingly bestowed during the progress of the Armada fight were all well won, and none more cLrduously than that of John Hawkins.

For Hawkins, the fireships at Calais (said to have been suggested by the Queen) were a reminder of his own experience at San Juan. The tables were now turned on the Spaniards full heartily, and the confusion occasioned by the advent of the eight blazing hulks far transcended, even allowing for the disparity in the number of ships involved, the excitement and horror of fire displayed by the English in the West Indies when this method of war had been initiated against them. While the great galleass, *Admiral*, of De Moçada went ashore on the sands of Calais and was assailed by Sir Amyas Preston in a longboat with a hundred men, while Drake, in the *Revenge*, with Fenner and the rest of the privateers, was setting about the Spanish fleet on the sea-ward side, Hawkins's division, led by the *Victory*, and including the *Swallow*, commanded by his son Richard, came down upon Sidonia's line and broke right through it, firing heavily and doing great damage. It is interesting to notice that the *Swallow* was the only English ship that received any great injury.

This was the final discomfiture of the invaders. After a council of war, with Oquendo anxious to fight on and Florez eager to fly, they made sail for the north. Hawkins and Drake accompanied Howard, who escorted the Spaniards past the Firth of Forth to make sure that no landing was attempted, and the English then returned south. The weather was again violent, and they were all much fatigued and suffering badly from shortness of provisions when Howard anchored off Margate, Hawkins dropped into Harwich, and the rest found shelter in the Downs. The tragedy of Margate and Harwich must be relegated to a later moment.

The campaign was over. Philip's great *empresa* had utterly failed. The Deliverance was accomplished, and the islanders were masters of the seas. The effect in England itself of the defeat of the Armada was extraordinary and wide-spreading; it gave a tremendous impetus to the national spirit; but the way in which the men were treated who accomplished the victory was a lamentable outrage. Not one of them suffered more than Hawkins. He had equipped the fleet and organised the crews; he had taken a valiant part in the hottest of the fighting. He was soon to know his reward.

It has been said that at this period love of Queen and country was a romantic passion among every rank of Englishmen. It was all that, and something more. It was a complete devotion to a high ideal. England, the English system, the English faith — all that the word England represented — as it appeared to the Elizabethan sailors and soldiers, statesmen and poets, was a light set on high to illumine a dark world, a beacon to which all the forces of progress might rally, a torch of freedom — freedom of mind, political freedom in a higher form than had been known since the Renaissance began, a degree of religious freedom high for the age. Above all, they were devoted to the resolute maintenance of national independence. National solidarity became a fact; national interests were unified; national heroes were elected. The atmosphere of the time favoured the development of the enthusiasm for adventure and discovery, and encouraged daring exploration in hitherto unknown worlds, widening knowledge and increasing wealth.

It was in these conditions that the great Elizabethan literature grew. The men who had made the old maps useless, and disclosed new fields whence the trader might draw new riches, the soldier new glory, and the poet new figures, were the men who had also opened the new social vista, along which eager eyes now wandered, by crushing ultramontane plots and destroying the aspirations of ecclesiastical tyrants, lay and clerical; who had released the nation, finally as it seemed, from the dread terror of a renewal of the priestly domination. They let in the bright light in which, for the remainder of the reign, English society developed and English literature flourished; they prised open the secrets of a new world in more than the bare material sense. They freed not only the limbs of Englishmen; not only did they free the seas to English keels; their bequest to the nation was beyond all measure of price. A glorious wave of progress in commerce, industry and the arts began with the destruction of the Armada and the overthrow of the obstacles that had held men's minds in the chains of serfdom, limiting their freedom of action, and checking by fire and sword all movement towards freedom of the intellect.

This is not too wide a view to take of the work of the seamen of England. But these men, loyal in the most perfect and honourable sense, devoted as they were to the national ideals, praying for the unity of the nation, and calling down confusion upon the heads of its enemies, were abominably treated by the Queen they served so zealously and honoured with an almost religious veneration. It speaks eloquently for the exalted spirit of the age that badgered and abused commanders did little more than grumble under their breath, that starving and half-naked sailors did not mutiny.

Hawkins, for a long time after this supreme effort had been expended, was the very picture of a good man struggling with adversity. He had exhausted himself, soul, mind, and body, in the public service. If he was not actually spurned by the Queen and her Ministers, his life was made a torment to him by neglect and lack of consideration, and by the callous manner in which impossible tasks were imposed on him and censure was administered because they proved impossible.

When the English had chased the Armada past the Firth of Forth, and the danger was over, their fleet was in piteous plight for lack of provisions and clothing. They had been fighting and pursuing for near three weeks; they were weary, battered, storm-tossed. The victuals distributed at Plymouth on the 23rd of June had been made to last seven weeks. The condition of Howard's men was nearly as bad as that of Medina Sidonia's, harassed by the enemy, driven ashore by the gale, made prisoners in Scotland or murdered in Ireland. The exceptions were that they were not on a hostile coast, that their ships were in perfect sea-trim thanks to Hawkins's long endeavours, and that they were exceptionally good seamen. The storm in the North Sea increased as they beat back southward, and before they could reach the mouth of the Thames the weather was so violent that the fleet became separated. Howard reached Margate, and Hawkins with his division, as already stated, went into Harwich.

On the 9th of August, when they got food, three days' rations given out as they turned back from the Scottish coast had been made to serve for over a week. The men were weak and wretched. The bad beer which had 3one so much damage at Plymouth was their only beverage; combined with short rations of salt beef and fish it produced an epidemic of sickness. At Margate, sailors were conveyed ashore and laid down in the streets to finish their mortal careers; there was no place in the town where they could be bestowed when all the barns and outhouses had been filled up with invalids. Howard and his officers were stricken with hopeless sorrow, having to look vainly on while their brave fellows perished like poisoned rats. Writing to Burghley on the 20th of August, Howard said, "It would grieve any man's heart to see men who had served so valiantly die so miserably." Thus England rewarded her heroes — did not pay them, did not feed them. The fever that took them to-day carried them off to-morrow; an immensely greater number died from this avoidable cause after the war was over than had fallen in the fighting with the Spaniards.

There never was a greater scandal in the conduct of any war than this. The Queen and Government did little to secure the victory that saved England; on the contrary they did what folly and cupidity could do to defeat their own cause. To the courage and devotion of the commanders and seamen alone did the nation owe the Great Deliverance. A sinister aspect is given to the attitude of the authorities towards the naval service in a letter from Hawkins that will call for more detailed consideration presently. He wrote to Cecil (August 26th): "Your Lordship may think that by death, discharging of sick, etc., something may be spared in the general pay. Those that died — their friends require their pay. For those which are discharged, we take on fresh men, which breeds a far greater charge." In the hour of victory, Elizabeth's principal thought was how much she could save by the death of the men, who, after gaining that victory, had been poisoned by villainous contractors, and starved by her own parsimony.

Chapter XVIII - Figures

Some insight has already been obtained into the nature of the office held by Hawkins as Controller and Treasurer of the fleet, the troubles and difficulties with which he was constantly confronted, and the inroads made upon his private purse by the demands of the service with which Elizabeth would not comply. Something has also been seen of the wavering, vacillating policy adopted in the months that preceded the Armada fight — the commissioning and laying up of ships, the engagement and discharge of sailors, the confusion into which the preparations were thrown. A great financial expert, with nothing else to do in life and a large staff to assist him, would have found the Treasurership a sufficient burden. Hawkins was not only treasurer, but constructor, controller, and fighting admiral. When the intricacies of the Queen's policy had tangled the naval accounts into an inextricable knot, Hawkins was called upon to take the *Victory* to sea and do the "donkey-work" for Howard. He did it right willingly, for seamanship and sea-fighting were his *métier.* But after a month's interlude, during which his distinguished skill and bravery earned him a knighthood, the web of the Treasurership began to close in upon him again. It was long before he emerged from the tangle that had been worked up for him by no fault of his own, in omission or commission, but by the follies of other people.

When Hawkins sailed into Harwich on his return from the north, on the 8th of August, 1588, he had with him nine of the Queen's ships, nine of the London privateers, three of the Plymouth contingent, two of the Dartmouth vessels, and a dozen others. They found some hoys there with bread and beer, and more victualling vessels arrived during the day. These Hawkins was to convoy to Howard's squadron. Within a few days he had seen the supplies to their destination. The weather continued wild. The ships at Margate had difficulty in communicating with the shore, and a part of them, including the *Ark Royal* and the *Victory,* went to Dover Roads. There, too, they experienced trouble in victualling the ships; small craft could hardly ply about the fleet for the violence of the wind and the force of the tides.

On August 24th, Cecil wrote to Howard requiring to be informed what number of mariners and soldiers were borne on the books of the fleet. Howard turned to Hawkins for the information, and on the 26th called him and Winter on board the flagship to advise. As the result of the interview, Hawkins wrote to Cecil the same day pointing out the difficulty of obtaining exact figures at that moment, with the southwesterly gale raging and the fleet divided. He stated that he and Drake on their own responsibility had discharged and sent home many of the ships of the Western volunteer fleet — an exercise in economy which had somewhat displeased Howard. He could not submit closer particulars of the numbers of men that were in her Majesty's pay than he had sent from Plymouth. He had then asked for £19,000, which would have brought the pay of the men up to the 28th of July. But that sum did not include many of the "voluntary ships" that had joined in the operations with the consent and by warrant of the Privy Council. He added a few unimportant details which he had been able to gather, and promised a fuller report when the weather should moderate.

Howard appended to the letter a memorandum, observing that Hawkins could do no more. As to the payment of the men who had done the Armada work, "God knoweth how they shall be paid except her Majesty have some consideration on them." A pretty exclamation to force a victorious Admiral to make about the men he had led to triumph! If he had to take money from his own purse (as, in fact, he did), Howard said he would see them paid.

But before this letter had reached him, Cecil was writing again to Hawkins in a querulous spirit of complaint. "I am sorry," said Sir John, replying to him, "I do live so long to receive so sharp a letter from your lordship, considering how carefully I take care to do all for the best and to cease charge." His one desire, he proclaimed, was to get this account square, and when that was done he hoped he would be relieved of the terrible duties of his offices. "I trust you will so provide for me that I shall never meddle with such intricate matters more...If I had any enemy, I would wish him no more harm than the course of my troublesome and painful life." It was a pathetic condition of mind for such a man with such a record. But Hawkins knew that man is born to trouble as the sparks fly upward: "hereunto, and to God's good providence, we are born.' He had shown the letter from Cecil to Howard and Winter; they, he said, were best able to judge of his care and painful travail, and of the efforts he was making to reduce the cost of the fleet. Elizabeth and the Council wanted impossibilities; they wanted not only to avoid the payment of the Navy for the work it had done, but also to reduce the current charges to a small minimum at once. Hawkins showed that the fleet had been decimated by the sickness caused by neglect and ill-treatment, and it was not possible to maintain the ships without engaging fresh men. Some, it was said, were left with hardly enough rags of a crew to lift anchor.

They continued to worry Sir John. They wanted statistics which, owing to the wobbling policy of the early year, it was impossible to gather; they wanted vouchers for everything. Until the first week in September, the fleet did not reassemble after its dispersal. The ships were all gathered in the Downs on the fifth of that month. Hawkins at once ferried from ship to ship, collecting the particulars that were wanted, and the same day sent word to Cecil that about 4,300 men were in the vessels still in commission. The burden of his life, adding the importunities of officers to the demands of the Government for greater economy, was becoming intolerable. "I would to God," he cried, in a letter to Walsingham, "I were delivered of the dealing for money." He was doing what man could do to get the crooked business straight, but he had no confidence that his protestations would be believed: he had painful experience of the lot of one who served a Queen who knew good men, but knew not how good men should be treated.

The completeness of the disaster that had attended Philip's enterprise was not realised by the Council, and Sir John had to point out how perilous it would be to allow the fleet to undertake any further operations in its present state. The ships wanted overhauling, reprovisioning, fresh manning. If Elizabeth wanted to put an end to the drain upon the Treasury, the way to do it was to lay up the ships and do all that was necessary to make them fit for service, to select vessels and men for a blockade of the Spanish coast, with raids on Spanish shipping, as he had suggested nearly a year before. In December, Edward Fenton, his brother-in-law, was appointed deputy to Hawkins, in order that the Treasurer might have more leisure to wrestle with the accounts. In eight months of laborious application he completed the task.

Everything was then made up to the previous December, and not a flaw could be discovered in Hawkins's honest dealing. A rogue would have made himself a wealthy man; Hawkins had laid a heavy hand on roguery wherever he found it, and had lost a great deal of money himself. When funds were not forthcoming for necessary things, he dipped into his own fortune: in thirteen years, from 1577 to 1590, he paid out of his pocket £9,659. "Continual thraldom," he called it, renewing his appeal to be released from office, but without avail.

Sir John Hawkins did not, however, allow himself to be obsessed by the wretched business of pulling the Navy accounts straight and endeavouring to get back the money that the Government owed to him. He was ever a friend of poor sailors, and one of his first proceedings after the Armada had been disposed of was to consider what could be done permanently to benefit the men who were disabled in the sea service. Although the loss of life by fighting in the contest with the Spaniards had not been heavy, and the proportion of wounded men was not great, the casualties were sufficient to direct a practical mind like that of Hawkins into the path of practical benevolence.

Two important naval institutions had their birth in his fatherly care for his mariners at this time. The first was the Greenwich Hospital Fund, which originated in "the Chest at Chatham," founded at the end of 1588 by Hawkins and Drake for the benefit of those seamen who had been wounded or incapacitated in the Armada, and of all seamen in the royal service who might thereafter be disabled while performing their duty. The idea was that seamen and shipwrights should every month voluntarily set aside a part of their pay as a contribution to the fund. It was put into practice for a long time, and incorporated with the Greenwich Hospital Fund when the royal palace by the riverside was appropriated to the purposes of a home for disabled seamen, long afterwards.

The business-like bent of Sir John Hawkins's mind is finely displayed in the establishment of the Chatham Chest; his personal generosity in the second of the two institutions referred to — the hospital at Chatham which he founded and endowed for the accommodation of poor decayed mariners and shipwrights. According to Hasted's "Kent," an inscription cut in the wall shows that the building was completed in 1592. A charter, still preserved, was granted to the charity by Queen Elizabeth in 1594. It defines the position of "the governors of the hospital of Sir John Hawkins, Knight, in Chatham." The number of governors was to be twenty-six, and at their head, "the Archbishop of Canterbury, the Bishop of Rochester, the Lord High Admiral, the Lord Warden of the Cinque Ports, the Dean of Rochester, the Treasurer, the Comptroller, Surveyor, and Clerk of Accounts of the Navy, six principal masters of mariners, two principal shipwrights, the Master and Wardens of Trinity House for the time being, and their successors," etc. The founder conveyed land and tithes for the endowment of the hospital. During his life he retained the right of appointing the beneficiaries; after his death the governors inherited it. No person could be received into the place who had not been "maimed, disabled, or brought to poverty," while in the naval service of England. There was accommodation for twelve pensioners, each of whom received a gratuity of two shillings a week. These were the inscriptions on the gate: on the outer side, "The poor you shall always have with you, to whom ye may do good if ye will"; and on the inner side, "Because there shall be ever some poor in the land, therefore I command thee, saying. Thou shalt open thine hand unto thy brother that is needy and poor in the land." The oak chest in which the Charter is preserved bears the arms of Hawkins.

In a character sketch in contrast between Hawkins and Drake, an anonymous contemporary left a picture of Hawkins which cannot be accepted without a good deal of reserve, for it describes him as "passing sparing, indeed miserable." No doubt his commercial training had made him careful of the guineas; but he was not miserly. These instances of his generosity towards poor seamen, and the state which, as we have seen, he kept on the *Jesus of Lubek,* are sufficient evidence to disprove the charge.

We hark back to 1588 — Hawkins struggling to hew some semblance of shapeliness out of an ugly mountain of figures, and longing all the time to be at sea. Sir John's son, Richard, was contemplating a voyage to the South Seas, examining and surveying unknown lands, and returning by Japan, China, and the East Indies; incidentally, he proposed to despoil King Philip of such treasure as might be met with, according to precedent now well established. He laid down in the Thames at the end of 1588 a large ship of between 300 and 400 tons, intended to take him upon this adventure. The design and construction were carried out under the immediate supervision of father and son, and embodied their ideal of a good ship. When finished, she was, as Richard said, "pleasing to the eye, profitable for stowage, good of sail, and well-conditioned." But this celebrated vessel never brought anything but disaster to the Hawkinses; it was in her that Richard carried out his unfortunate voyage to the Pacific; it was to release or avenge his son, captured by the Spaniards while fighting in her, that John Hawkins set out on his last fatal adventure.

The ship was launched by Lady Hawkins, and to the consternation of everybody concerned, and particularly of Richard, she named her the *Repentance.* An uncouth name, exclaimed her son, expostulating with her; but Lady Hawkins replied that "repentance was the safest ship they could sail in to purchase the haven of Heaven." She did not retain the title long. Passing in her barge to the palace of Greenwich one day, Queen Elizabeth saw the beautiful ship riding at anchor in the river, and desired to be rowed round her. From post to stem and waterline to truck, everything pleased the Queen but the name; imperiously she declared that she would christen the ship anew, and named her the *Dainty.*

Richard commanded the *Dainty* in the next expedition organised by Sir John — a raid on the coast of Spain. The Admiral had been expecting to start in 1589, and had made much preparation at great expense, with the usual result, that he was delayed for a year. He could not get out of Elizabeth what she owed him — over £2,000 in connection with the Armada expenses, £7,000 his share of the last adventure with Drake, and £700 in connection with the equipment of the *Repentance;* nor could he get his warrant for the new voyage till the following May (1590). The Queen's commission then granted authorised him to press and take up men for her service, for manning his own ship the *Mary Rose,* and the remainder of the fleet of fourteen vessels provided, one division being under the command of Hawkins himself and the other under Sir Martin Frobisher, in the *Revenge.* It was stipulated that he should not make aggression against the ships of any Power with which England was on terms of friendship.

The voyage, which commenced towards the close of the summer, was not highly successful. The project was to intercept the Plate fleet, but the Spaniards had warning of that intention, and were able to avoid the English force by keeping their treasure ships on the other side of the Atlantic. In vain did Hawkins he in wait for them at Flores. That western sentinel of the Azores afforded him excellent shelter for his ships, but no Spaniards came by. The fleet returned to England in December, carrying in to Dartmouth the only vessel that had been captured, and the financial results of the enterprise were not so large as had been expected. The fate of the Armada had made the Spaniards timorous about meeting the English at sea. For the most part they kept in harbour.

The one great chance that the English had was not taken. It was in this way — the story is related by Richard Hawkins. The fleet was off Finisterre one morning, when hove in sight eight Spanish men-of-war, taking ammunition and provisions to the Due de Mercoeur, then engaged in hostilities with Henry IV. in Brittany. The Vice-admiral, Frobisher — and apparently this was contrary to Sir John's orders — was some twelve or fifteen miles ahead of the Admiral's division at the time. Frobisher gave chase, and the Spaniards fled, making for the harbour of Mungia (Mugia, a few miles from Finisterre). Richard Hawkins almost came up with the particular vessel he was pursuing, but the whole eight of them got clean away in the end. There was, however, some pretty smart fighting, and the Spaniards lost 200 men. Richard declared, with filial loyalty, that if Frobisher had been in his place, and the operations had been under the direction of Sir John, the result would have been different. It is impossible to estimate the chances on the evidence that exists. The fact remains that Hawkins was criticised on account of the meagre harvest he brought home. He told Elizabeth that "Paul doth plant, Apollo doth water; but God giveth the increase." The Queen's retort was full-bodied, even for the taste of the time: "God's death! This fool went out a soldier and is come home a divine!"

There were some disputes about the division of the spoils on board the Biscayan, which had been taken into Dartmouth, and in 1592 the quarrel was renewed when the *Madre de Dios,* the largest prize ever brought to England, was sailed into the same port. Hawkins had a share in the famous expedition that resulted in this capture, the profits of which were rumoured to be £500,000, and were certainly well over £150,000.

Chapter XIX - The Dainty

Many events were crowded into the seven years of Hawkins's life after the defeat of the Armada. They were hardly happy years. Personal sorrows visited him in the death of his brother William, to whose memory he erected a monument in Deptford Church, and, in 1591, in the death of his wife Katharine. He married again. His second wife, Margaret, one of the Queen's women of the bedchamber, daughter of Charles Vaughan, of Hergest, was, however, in poor health, and was always practically a prisoner in her house at Deptford, though she survived him twenty years. The last great blow was to fall in 1593.

Hawkins had obtained for his son Richard a commission from the Queen for a voyage with "ship, bark, and pinnance" to the West Indies and the South Seas. The *Dainty,* it will be remembered, had been built for that purpose. The adventurers were to have all they could take from King Philip, with the usual reservation that one-fifth of the treasure, jewels, and pearls should be given to the Queen.

The delays were more vexatious even than before. There was talk of an expedition to Nombre de Dios and across the Isthmus to Panama, to capture the treasure train; a great deal of such talk had come to nothing. Plenty of time was given for the surreptitious friends of Philip in England to communicate to Spain all the details of young Hawkins's proposal and his equipment. Philip sent messengers of warning West to prepare his representatives in the islands and on the Continent for the coming of the Englishmen, who did not start till the summer of 1593. The *Dainty* was prepared in the Thames, and taken down Channel to Plymouth, where the other ships were waiting. Of these, the *Fancy* was commanded by Captain Robert Tharlton; the *Hawke* and the pinnace were both contributed by Richard Hawkins, in addition to the *Dainty.* A May gale rooted the mainmast out of the big ship and drove the pinnace ashore in the Sound, and a fortnight was occupied in repairing damages. Friends told Richard Hawkins that these were ill omens; his wife — his "truest friend and second self" — seemed to have a presentiment of the evil to follow; with tears she begged him to abandon the voyage or send some other mariner in his stead. But this was an affair of notoriety all over England; many eyes were upon him, and he "shut the door of all impediment" and closed his ears against all contrary counsel.

Richard Hawkins — the "Almirante Ricardo" of the Spaniards — was as popular a personage in Plymouth as his father had been. He was a freeman of the town, a member of the commonalty, a contributor to all local causes, and had recently provided "four demy-culverins and three sakers" for the defences of the town. Not merely for his gifts of nine-pounders and five-pounders, not only for his public merit in other respects was Captain Richard beloved; he was as genial and delightful as a brave man and a skilled seaman and a daring soldier could be. All Plymouth went to the Hoe on the afternoon of the 12th of June, when he passed out, not to return again for close upon ten years. They gathered "to show their grateful correspondency of the love and zeal which I, my father, and our predecessors have ever borne to that place as to our natural and mother town." With blowing of trumpets and firing of artillery from ship and shore they made their way across the Sound, and the last echoes of the impressive farewell did not die away till night fell.

The voyage was unlucky from the first. The Spaniards had been warned and were wary, and only tolerable success in the capture of prizes met them all the way across the Atlantic and South to the River Plate. At a Brazilian port, they tried without success the trading tactics which Sir John had introduced at Burboroata twenty years before. Off the mouth of the Plate, Tharlton, in the *Fancy,* deserted and returned to England. As the *Hawke* had been found an incumbrance, and they had burnt her, Hawkins was now left with only one ship and a pinnace to accomplish the rest of his long and perilous voyage. He said some short sentences about Tharlton, and went on to the south. He rediscovered the Falkland Islands, which had been found previously — though the fact was unknown to him — by Davis. He named the place "Hawkins's Maiden-Land" — "for that it was discovered in the reign of Queen Elizabeth, my sovereign lady and mistress and a maiden queen, and at my cost and adventure, in perpetual memory of her chastity and remembrance of my endeavours." He sailed through the Straits of Magellan, and up the Pacific coast of America, making some captures in the port of Valparaiso. News of Hawkins's presence on the coast was circulated rapidly, and, a squadron of six ships sent against him having failed ignominiously to take the *Dainty,* a squadron of eight, with 1,500 men under Don Beltran de Castro, was despatched. Hawkins had seventy-five men, all told. The fight that followed was probably, next to that of the *Revenge* under Grenville, the most desperate one-sided conflict in all the history of sea-fighting. For three days and three nights the doomed ship *Dainty* sustained a continual bombardment of great guns and a ceaseless fusillade of musketry. Attempt after attempt to board and take the vessel was beaten off with great gallantry. Hawkins was himself wounded in six places on the first day, and two of his hurts were serious.

The captain of the *Dainty* urged him to surrender, the odds being so great and their numbers little by little decreasing. Hawkins indignantly declined to consider the suggestion. He recalled to him the fact that many Englishmen who had surrendered to the Spaniards had been treacherously treated. He reminded him of the great betrayal at San Juan, and of the fate of John Oxenham and his men, who, having surrendered upon a compromise, were taken to Lima and hanged for pirates. He urged "constancy" — "Let us as Englishmen sell our lives dearly in battle rather than die the death that the Inquisition may decree." Catching the spirit of his leader, the *Dainty's* captain vowed to fight it out; the men were heartened by the courage of their officers. Night brought no cessation of the struggle: only at dawn the combatants drew breath while they took counsel for another deadly day's work. For another day and night, and yet another day, the cannonade went on. The *Dainty's* sails were torn to shreds, her masts were disabled, her pumps were shot to pieces, she had fourteen shots below the water-line, and seven or eight feet of water in her hold. About thirty of her men had been killed, and nearly all the rest were wounded. Then Hawkins gave consent to surrender before the ship went down. He stipulated for the lives and liberties of all his men; on that condition only was the surrender given; "otherwise we would die fighting." The Spanish Admiral sent Hawkins his glove as a pledge that they should be received *à buena guerra,* and swore that they should be sent as speedily as possible into England.

Doubtless Don Beltran meant what he said. He received Hawkins with Castilian courtesy, accommodating him in his own cabin, and did what he could to ease the sufferings of the men. So they were carried into Panama. There Don Beltran was able to show one of the letters that had unfolded Hawkins's scheme to Philip before the expedition started. The Spaniard treated the redoubtable "Ricardo" with kindness, as befitted the conqueror in a fight so uneven, a fight of which Sir John must have read the story with a tingling of the blood. Don Beltran's prisoner on parole was far too badly hurt to be able to write himself, but he dictated to his servant an account of what had happened, for transmission to his father. Thus the news became known in England. The prisoners were taken to Lima. Gradually it appeared that the Spanish authorities did not intend to keep Don Beltran's promise to release them.

When this was made clear to the eyes of those at home, the old man was deeply affected. He could endure no longer the torments of his official life. Misfortune had dogged his latter days. This final blow at him through the person of his only son was more than he could bear in a state of inaction. Prompted by the thought that Richard was possibly in the hands of the Inquisition, remembering San Juan and what had happened to some of his men who had been left with the Spaniards there, and especially to his own master, Robert Barret, realising the torture that this thing meant for his son's wife Judith at Plymouth — he planned his last expedition. He would take a large force, see whether he could not compel the King of Spain to keep the promise of his representative, and, if not, take vengeance in his own way. Drake joined him. The idea was approved by the Queen and the Privy Council, and it soon began to excite men's minds very highly throughout the country. It was the talk of all the sea-ports and the theme of the balladists, who urged the adventurous youth of England to join her "Nestor and Neptune" in this enterprise. This very year had been published Spenser's picture of Hawkins in Colin Clout's account of his excursion into the great world of London:

"And Proteus eke with him does drive his herd
  Of stinking seals and porpoises together;
With hoary head and dewy-dropping beard,
  Compelling them which way he list and whether."

Very minor poets celebrated him also. "The Trumpet of Fame," an exceedingly curious pamphlet in rhyme, was published while the fleet was fitting out. It had for a secondary title, "Sir Francis Drake's and Sir John Hawkins's Farewell: With an encouragement to all Sailors and Soldiers that are minded to go in this worthy enterprise. With the names of many ships, and what they have done against our foes." It appealed for support for the adventurers in this fashion:

"Drake, conquering Drake...
  A friend to friends, a scourge unto the foe,
  A plague for those that wish sweet England's woe.

"Be forward, then, and joy in this brave Knight,
  That never yet received foil in fight;
  But still return'd with fame and wealth away.
  In spite of those that would the same gainsay.

"And Hawkins, in this action his compeer.
  Full well is known a famous cavalier.
  Whose valour shown, and service often done,
  With good success immortal fame hath won."

The notes of the "Trumpet" are something throaty; they are re-sounded to show the character of the interest excited by the expedition. An account was also published of Drake's voyage of 1572, having been collated by the Rev. P. Nicholls from the narrative of men who sailed with him.

Hawkins drew out a scheme, and saw to the perfection of all the preparations. It was in connection with this work that the opinion of Sir Thomas Gorges, already quoted, was given: "Sir John Hawkins is an excellent man in these things: he sees all things done orderly." Part of the cost of the expedition was borne by private adventurers — mostly by Drake and Hawkins themselves — and part by the State. Sir John was the chief contributor: his share of the expenses amounted to £18,662, and Drake's to £12,842. The royal ships engaged were the *Garland, Defiance, Bonaventure, Hope, Foresight,* and *Adventure.* There were twenty-one other vessels, and the total force at the command of Drake and Hawkins, who were in joint commission, was 2,500 men and boys. While they were waiting at Plymouth for the word to start, a diversion was created by the arrival of four Spanish galleys off the Cornish coast to the west of Penzance, where they landed soldiers and did

119

some damage. An express was sent to Hawkins and Drake for assistance. Finally, they got away on August 28th, 1595.

Sir John had made his will in the previous year, and now added a codicil, written in special view of the fate of his son Richard, whom he was going to seek. It set forth that in the original document he had appointed his wife and his son as executors, but now, "forasmuch as the said Richard Hawkins is supposed to be taken and detained prisoner in the Indies," he proposed, if Richard did not return to England within three years from December 20th, 1595, the widow should be sole executrix, and at least £3,000 should be devoted to the ransom of his son.

It was patent that a project so great, and advertised so extensively in England, must be well known to the King of Spain. As a matter of fact, he was informed of it months before the fleet's departure, and made his arrangements accordingly. He sent news to every part of his dominions likely to be affected, and in order to gain further time, his agents raised the report that another Armada was being got ready to invade England. The ruse was so far successful that the fleet was kept hanging about Plymouth long after Hawkins had intended to be off. Before they left England, the two Admirals had information that a wealthy galleon had been separated from the Plate fleet, and the Queen was anxious that they should attempt to capture it. In this circumstance lay the germ of failure. Hawkins desired to devote the strength of the fleet to the performance of the Queen's wish, and to proceed at once in search of the galleon in question, which, owing to the loss of a mast, had been obliged to return to Puerto Rico. Drake was of another opinion. He and Hawkins were of equal authority; the dispute which arose was an instance of the evils of dual control. Hawkins allowed himself to be overborne by the weight of Drake's opinion, since he was backed by Sir Thomas Baskerville, who commanded the military side of the expedition. Thus valuable time was lost in a fruitless invasion of the Canaries, and in refitting at Dominica. This was all Philip wanted — time. He was able to complete his arrangements for strengthening the defences of Nombre de Dios and Panama, upon which, it was known, an attack was meditated; and, with regard to the rich galleon at Porto Rico, he sent across five big warships to defend her.

The old Sea Dog, now sixty-three, and grown grizzled in the service of Elizabeth's Navy, was not, this August, the vigorous and buoyant man who had sailed from Plymouth on his last thrilling voyage to the West Indies twenty years before. He had won much glory. He had done much good work. Fortune had, to a certain extent, smiled upon his worldly estate. But he had suffered severely from the pains of a thankless office; family uprootings had shaken him, and the anxiety he felt about the fate of his son made him greyer, deepened the furrows on his dark face. It was with some sorrowful apprehension of a long journey into the unknown that, on Thursday, the 28th of August, he took leave of his daughter-in-law. Mistress Judith, and her child, promising to do what, in his paternal solicitude, he could to restore husband and father to them.

The fine fleet worked out of harbour that afternoon, and anchored for the night in Cawsand Bay. Next day they bade farewell to the Devonshire coast and set their course south-west. The cliffs about Plymouth

Sound sank down into the sea, and the conical peak of Rame vanished also. The Dartmoor hills followed them. Neither Hawkins nor Drake was ever to see those familiar landmarks again. Within a few months both were resting their last rest far below the gleaming surface of the Caribbean Sea.

Chapter XX - The Bitter End

As though to warn them of the irretrievable disasters which this voyage was to bring, they began to meet with misfortune as soon as they started. Baskerville's ship, the *Hope,* ran up on the Eddystone Reef as they worked out into the Channel, but was got off without serious damage. They stood down to Finisterre, but did nothing on the Spanish coast, and for the first month were lacking adventure. They took two small Flemish fly-boats on the 8th of September, extracted what information they could from them, and let them go.

By this time Drake's Canary Island scheme had been agreed upon, Hawkins reluctantly consenting against his better judgment; and they rose the islands on the 26th. On the 27th they anchored off Grand Canary, about three miles from the fort. This was well-known ground to Hawkins; the traders of the Canaries were old friends of his; it was improbable that he had any enthusiasm for the proceedings, and he had at the back of his mind the conviction that they were wasting time and jeopardising the main object of their voyage. He was eager to be off to the Western Ocean. However, Drake took the responsibility and the direction of these operations. His plan was to land some fourteen hundred men on the sandy beach between the fort and the town, and he began, as soon as the anchors were down, to make preparations to that end. But he found that the news of his coming had preceded him; the Spaniards were apprehensive of trouble, and had made ready to meet him and to contest the invasion with all their available strength. They hurriedly threw up earthworks on the land behind the beach — which was the only practicable landing-place — and dug trenches in which their arquebussiers were posted. Altogether, they displayed a force of about nine hundred, horse and foot.

The English sent several of their smaller ships in within musket-shot of the shore to cover the landing. The vessels engaged in this service were the *Solomon,* the *Bonaventure,* the *Elizabeth,* the *Constance,* the *Phoenix,* the *Ivell,* the *Littlejohn,* the *Delight,* the *Pegasus,* the *Exchange,* the *Francis,* a caravel, and two small ketches. With the force thus represented, and Drake's military skill and determination to aid it, there is no doubt that the landing could have been effected if the circumstances had been favourable, and the Spanish

121

horse and foot would have been as impotent as the Treasurer's little army at Rio de la Hacha which Hawkins had dispersed so easily on a similar occasion many years before. But the circumstances were not favourable. Never an Englishman set foot on shore. The beach was a very hot place with the trenches behind it. Drake's pikemen might have cleared them if they could have landed without losing half their number. The difficulty was in landing. The sea beat furiously on the beach; it would have required very delicate negotiation even if there had been no opposition; as it was, there was no chance. Reluctant to give in, Drake went inshore himself in his barge to examine the situation. At once he decided against the attempt and ordered the ships out of range; it would have been folly to persist. He was rarely beaten, but he was not so foolish as not to know when he was beaten.

The whole fleet then stood away to the west end of the island, where the ships watered. They encountered great hostility, even in this remote district. Captain Grimston ventured to ascend a hill, near which the ships lay, in the company of several officers and men, and was attacked by herdsmen. Grimston and three or four of his men were killed in a curious fight, in which the islanders set their dogs upon the English and assailed them with staves. All the rest were wounded, and the surgeon of the *Solomon* was taken prisoner. It was alleged against him that under pressure from the Spaniards he disclosed the plans of Hawkins and Drake, and that the Governor of the Canaries sent a caravel off at once to the West Indies to warn the authorities of the ports which the privateers intended to visit. But, as Captain Savile, who tells the story of the voyage, remarks, there was no need for this. Such a fuss had been made in England about the expedition that Philip had been able to advise his deputies in the far West three weeks before the squadron sailed from Plymouth. A Flemish merchant, also, who had been in London and seen something of the great preparations for the equipment of *Nestor and Neptune,* had carried the news to the West Indies far in advance of the ships themselves.

Time had thus been wasted. It would have been far better if Drake had consented to adopt John Hawkins's plan. They sailed from the Canaries on the 28th, a Sunday, bidding farewell to the inhospitable islands late at night, and directing their course to the west, with sorrowful hearts for the fruitless loss of their comrades, and some misgivings about their success. They were about a month crossing the Atlantic. As usual, they fetched the Windward Islands first, sighting Martinique on the 27th of October. The weather was very stormy, and on the night of the 26th, Drake, with five or six ships, was separated from the rest of the fleet, and stood for Dominica. Owing to the violence of the gale, he altered his course still further, and, while Hawkins was going round the south of Dominica, went north to the little isle of Marie Galante. He anchored on the 28th on the north-east side of the island, and went ashore in his barge, meeting with a canoeful of Caribs from Dominica, with whom he bartered "a yellow waistcoat of flannel and a handkerchief" for such fruits as they had. On the 29th he weighed to meet Hawkins, sailing among the islets of Todos Santos (now the lies des Saintes) and anchored off the south-east coast of Guadeloupe, where Hawkins joined him with all his ships but one.

That one had a tragic fate; and its tragedy had an important bearing on the still greater tragedy that was to follow. On the 30th, the *Francis,* a little vessel of thirty-five tons, being the rearmost of Hawkins's squadron, fell among five of the Spanish frigates sent by King Philip to protect the treasure at Puerto Rico. It was a hapless encounter. The little English ship might possibly have shown the Spaniards clean heels, and have got away to join the rest of the fleet, but for a misunderstanding. She mistook them for her consorts, and cordially closed up to them, till, discovering that they were enemies, she found it too late to save herself. She put up a fight, but was simply overwhelmed by numbers and metal. Only one English vessel was in sight, impotent to help, a caravel ahead of her which witnessed the battle and the disaster. The *Francis* was quickly silenced and captured, and most of her crew were taken on board the Spanish ships as prisoners of war and transported to Puerto Rico. Among them was John Austin, of whom we hear later. It is related that when the *Francis* was abandoned to the mercy of the wind and sea, there were left in her three or four sick and wounded men — an act of inhumanity said to have been confessed by Spaniards whom the English afterwards took at Puerto Rico.

This loss was not a great thing, but it affected Hawkins very deeply. The blow to his prestige seemed hard for him to bear; further, the incident seemed to foreshadow the failure to which the whole enterprise was doomed. The presence of these numerous Spanish warships in the neighbourhood, alert and aggressive, was the first definite intimation they had that their arrival and their plans were known to the colonial authorities. They had reckoned upon surprising San Juan de Puerto Rico, but all hope of anything like a surprise was now out of the question. They would have to attack a stronghold fortified and prepared to meet them. The old admiral knew that he was right when he advised that, on leaving England, they should make for the West Indies direct and assail at once the treasure which they hoped to make their prey. He had given way to Drake, and it seemed to him that their misfortune was the immediate result. It is clear that the misunderstanding between these two was a sore trial to both of them. Hawkins began to show the effects of the disappointment at once; his men noticed that he was low-spirited and weak from the day when the dire news of the *Francis* arrived.

The fleet remained some days off Guadeloupe, riding close to the shore. They careened and cleaned some of the ships, foul after their two months' voyage; they sent their soldiers ashore to stretch their limbs and get military exercise; they put their pinnaces together They unloaded the *Richard,* a victualler, distributed her cargo throughout the fleet, dismantled her, and sent her to the bottom. They were then ready to depart. Reaching out from the shelter of Guadeloupe with a cloud of sail — the royal ships leading, and the privateers following, the newly equipped pinnaces scouting on the wings — they looked a formidable force as they reached away north-west, sailing upon the inner side of the Leeward Islands. By the 8th of November they were within measurable distance of their objective, Puerto Rico.

Hawkins had been getting worse, and was by this time very ill indeed. He kept his bed on board the *Garland* while they rode at anchor among the Virgin Islands, the men fishing with hook and line to vary their rations, or fowling on shore. On the 12th, they emerged to the north of the islands, and wore round to the west for Puerto Rico. Passing Culebra in the afternoon, they sighted Cape San Juan before nightfall. There, "at the easternmost end of St. John...Sir John Hawkins departed this life."

So, simply, is the great sailor's taking off described. Thus, within call of the guns of San Juan, came the end of the long career.

He had won his first fame in those latitudes thirty-two years before. Hispaniola, the scene of his first adventure, was a few leagues to the west of the spot where, that November evening, he closed his eyes upon the ships and the sea. Sad as it was, there was something fitting in the circumstance of his death. To have lived longer would have been but to witness the ghastliest failure that had ever attended an English armada in the seas to which he had shown the way. He was sixty-three; he had lived an arduous life, full of dangerous adventure, hard fighting, and hard work. Years had begun to tell upon him, and he was suffering from the intolerable strain of his official labours before he left England. He was staggered by the news about his son. The voyage was a vexation and a disaster from the first; he was deeply troubled about the disagreement with his colleague Drake. The accumulation of misfortunes was more than his worn and wearied body and his troubled mind could withstand. The loss of the *Francis* was the last touch of adversity needed to weigh down the mortal balance. Which grief of all killed John Hawkins it is useless to inquire; as Prince observes, "When the same heart hath two mortal wounds given it together, it is hard to say which of them killeth."

The officers and men of the fleet were cast into black sorrow by the death of Hawkins, and Drake most of all. His old kinsman had been his mentor first and his admirer after — for the pupil had exceeded even the fame of the master, and Hawkins never grudged the honours that Drake won. Recall his words to Bolland, when he could not join a proposed expedition himself, that adventurers could not be lacking for any enterprise in which Drake was concerned. Between two such men there must have been, in spite of all differences of opinion, a high and mutual respect and affection.

The old Sea Dog was committed to the sea within sound of the Spanish guns, with all the traditional honours, with all the solemnity of a mariner's funeral. Barnfield wrote in his epitaph:

"The waters were his winding-sheet,
    The sea was made his tomb;
Yet for his fame the ocean-sea

Was not sufficient room."

The story of the fateful adventure may be completed in a few words. Within less than three months Drake had followed his old friend upon his last long voyage. Upon the death of Hawkins, Sir Thomas Baskerville took his place in the *Garland,* and the same evening the fleet anchored off San Juan. Drake showed too great a contempt for the enemy. He lay within reach of the guns on shore, and, as he was at supper aboard his flagship, they opened fire upon the fleet. Two shots struck the ship — the first of which entered the great cabin, killed Sir Nicholas Clifford, mortally wounded Brute Browne and others, and knocked over the stool on which Drake himself was sitting. They had to haul off till morning, when they found that the Spaniards had sunk a ship at the entrance to the harbour, to prevent the ingress of the English fleet. Then Drake decided on a landing, and bade goodbye to Browne, who was at the point of death. "Ah, dear Brute," said he, "I could grieve for thee, but now is no time to let down my spirits." Drake carried San Juan by storm, with great loss to the Spaniards, but with little gain to himself, for the treasure had been taken away. The Spaniards had cleared the town of women and children and had everything ready for a vigorous defence.

Seeing that there was nothing to be done by remaining there, after a few days the admiral weighed for the Spanish Main. He took La Hacha and other places, but the results were still disappointing, and Drake began to suffer acutely from the sense of melancholy failure. He had never been his own man since he lost Hawkins. At Nombre de Dios they obtained some treasure. An expedition across the Isthmus, with Panama as its goal, led by Baskerville, was a dismal breakdown, and the English suffered great loss during the desultory fighting among the hills. After struggling half-way across they came back distressed, beaten, decimated. This was the blow that completed Drake's misery. He immediately fell ill of a fever, lingered three weeks, and died while the fleet was passing between Porto Bello and Escudo, on the 28th of January, 1596. "He used some speeches at, or a little before, his death, rising and apparelling himself; but, being brought to bed again, within one hour he died." They buried him at sea.

Baskerville, who now took charge of the fleet, had some fighting with the Spaniards before he got clear of the Indies, and the ships struggled home to Plymouth about the beginning of May. A Spanish account of the expedition was written by the Admiral, Don Bernaldino Delgadillo de Avelleneda, in which it was stated that *"Francisco Draque murio en Nombre de Dios, de pena de aver perdido tantos baxeles y gente."* Captain Savile, with Baskerville's approval, answered this in a long manifesto, denying that the losses inflicted upon him by the Spaniards had anything to do with the death of Drake. Baskerville, indeed, challenged Avelleneda to a duel "with whatsoever arms he shall make choice of" if he dared to reassert his slanders. There was a furious battle of words. The English were justly indignant about some of the Spanish Admiral's boasts as to the results of their encounters with him; but, so far as

Drake was concerned, there could be no doubt that the disappointments of the voyage hastened his death, as they had quickened the end of Hawkins. In fact, the whole story was regarded in England as calamitous, and its chief calamity was the loss of England's two greatest sailors.

Both Hawkins and Drake were deeply mourned by the whole nation when the news arrived. It was not until the end of March that a war-stained sailor came home to Plymouth who was able to report the death of Sir John. This was the John Austin already mentioned. He had been on board the *Francis* when she was taken by the Spaniards, and carried into San Juan de Puerto Rico. During the attack on that town, he was informed, Hawkins had been killed. The rumour held good till the fact became known a month later, when Cecil heard from Plymouth that both the admirals were dead, and received a description of the manner of their passing.

We left Richard Hawkins, whose woes were the inspiration of his father's last voyage, in the hands of the Spaniards at Lima. A captive when the old man set out from Plymouth, Richard remained interned till nearly two years after his father's death. Ere the news had reached Europe, Philip, unknowing the fate of the two adventurers he most dreaded, was writing to the Marquis of Cañete, Viceroy of Peru, about the treatment of the son of "Achines de Plimua." His letter is dated December 17th, 1595:

"I have felt much satisfaction on receiving the news of the success which De Castro obtained over the English General Ricardo, who entered that sea by the Strait of Magellan...As regards the punishment of the general and others who were captured in the said ship, you inform me that they have been claimed by the Inquisition, but that as you had no instructions from me as to their disposal, you have put off compliance with the requisition of the Holy Office, and the delivery of the said general to the auto. You understand that he is a person of quality. In this matter I desire that justice may be done conformably to the quality of the persons."

If Cañete had informed the King of the circumstances in which Richard Hawkins was taken, this was a most disingenuous letter. The English Admiral had surrendered only on condition that the lives of himself and his men should be spared and that they should be restored to England at the earliest possible moment. The sequel was almost a worse treachery than that which his father had suffered at San Juan de Ulloa. Spanish promises, once more, proved lying deceits. Until the arrival of the king's letter, there was danger of the Inquisition; indeed, one of Richard Hawkins's companions was sent by the Holy Office to the galleys at Nombre Dios, where he died. The Inquisition, which had burnt Robert Barret at Seville twenty years before, had been the terror of John Hawkins's soul while he irked under the delays that attended his setting forth from Plymouth on the voyage of vengeance; it was what Dame Judith at home feared most poignantly. As a matter of fact, Richard escaped the toils of the holy butchers by means of Philip's favour, such as it was, and by the admiration which his own valour and dauntless spirit aroused in the minds of his gaolers. Cañete treated him with signal kindness; the man who had made such a tremendous fight against odds was the Hon of the hour at Lima, and was allotted a fine house for his residence. He had been claimed by the Inquisition, it was true, and taken for a brief time to the "Holy House"; but these attentions ceased upon the arrival of the king's letter.

After two years he was sent into Spain, and still detained a prisoner, notwithstanding de Castro's solemn promise. De Castro himself protested as loudly as anybody, but his protests had no power to unbar the gates of the Castle of Seville. Richard's captivity lasted nearly ten years, and he was finally released through the good offices of the Count of Miranda, who said that, if a prisoner was detained when his liberty had been promised, no future agreement could be made because faith in Spanish honour would be destroyed.

Queen Elizabeth had treated John Hawkins scandalously enough. The heritage of neglect descended upon his son. He had a wife and child in England, and he was devoted to Dame Judith, remaining faithful to her against all the wiles of a Spanish señora who fell violently in love with him. He wrote from his prison in Spain imploring the Queen to secure his release, and reminding her of the services which for many years his father and himself had rendered to her and to the English Navy. Yet nothing serious was done. John Hawkins had left in his will £3,000 for the ransom of his son; not until the latter had been almost a decade in prison and had reached middle age was the other £9,000 provided to make up the total of the price set upon him by Spain. Richard Hawkins came home in January, 1603, two months before the Queen died. He came to find his father dead, his inheritance dissipated, his wife ten years older, his child Judith, whom he had left an infant, a girl of eleven. He set himself the task of restoring the family fortunes, and he succeeded. He was knighted by King James, to whom he applied for the forcible repair of the wrongs done to him by the Spaniards. He was elected Member of Parliament for Plymouth, and appointed Vice-Admiral of Devon; he lived a long and useful life — and died a disappointed man, as his father had died. His death occurred in 1622, when he was engaged upon the business of an expedition against the Algerine pirates, and it was said that he was killed by vexation because of the failure of the king to provide efficiently for the needs of the case. He suffered from the pusillanimity of James precisely as his father had suffered from the avarice and callousness of Elizabeth.

With the death of Hawkins and Drake in 1596, the most stirring chapter of the conflict between the English seamen and the power of Spain was closed. Other expeditions were fitted out — that of Essex to Cadiz, those of Sir Anthony Shirley and William Parker of Plymouth to the West Indies, involving the sack of Campeachy and the capture of Porto Bello. But the follies of Philip II. had ruined the glory of Spain, and after his death in 1598 their deteriorating, demoralising influence was felt to the full. Spanish fleets had been beaten at sea, the great Armada had been annihilated, the reputation of the Spanish soldiery had been buried in the marshes of the Low Countries. Not much was remaining for the English to fight when Philip's weak successor concluded his peace with James I. English adventurers turned their attention to other quarters of the globe, and particularly to the East Indies, where John Hawkins's nephew, William, son of his brother William, played a notable part in the foundation of our Oriental Empire.

Chapter XXI - Characteristics

The place in history of "the very wise, vigilant, and true-hearted man" who was committed to the deep off the coast of Puerto Rico can only be estimated properly in a view of the comparative state of England and Spain at the time of his entry into the world of action, and at his sad departure from it. Such a task is beyond the scope of this volume. It must suffice to say that he had no small share in the national movement that stirred all England so deeply in the latter half of the sixteenth century. In the first place, he established the important principle of the freedom of the sea to the ships of all nations, denied by the Spaniards in their regulations for the exclusion of all but Spanish keels from the Gulf of Mexico. Next, he was one of the first and most influential of the English privateers who, in the illicit war with Spain, dared greatly for something more than gold and glory, demonstrated the pluck and skill of the islanders, and with the policy of pin-pricks helped to erode the power of Philip, to expose the weaknesses that underlay its pride, and to explode its pretensions, — the claims that aroused Raleigh's scorn when he wrote: "They pretend title: as if the Kings of Castile were the natural heirs of the world!" Again, in the long preparation for the vital conflict of 1588, he showed fine qualities of administrative statesmanship as well as ingenuity of invention and seamanlike foresight, and proved a good man at a time when his failure would have been disastrous for England.

The Spanish banner flew in undisputed sovereignty over a great part of the world, and over all the New World, in 1563, when John Hawkins set out on his first voyage to the West Indies — when he "sailed over the ocean sea unto the Island of Hispaniola." That adventure was the first shock given to Spanish security in those latitudes. When Hawkins died in 1595, the dream of the subjugation of the Protestant heretics was over, sea supremacy had been transferred from Spain to England, and the Netherlands were soon to be freed from the yoke of Spain. Hawkins's ships and the ships of the men who were his compatriots and disciples had done this thing. Without sea supremacy the Reformation would never have been consummated, and Philip would inevitably have added the realm of England to the vast heritage left him by Charles V.

John Hawkins was a great administrator. It has been shown that his naval policy foreshadowed much that has since been worked into the body of the

English naval system. He was a great merchant — cool, calculating, successful. He was a considerable fighter, though he had a strange contempt for land soldiers. But he was greatest of all as a sailor.

"John Hawkyns, Marynr," is the title that best becomes him. His devotion to the profession of the sea, and his skill in it, became a proverb in his own time. Blue water was his native element. It called him away from the creeks of Plymouth, away from the Channel and its ports, and he obeyed the call, following it into oceans hitherto unknown to English eyes. He lived on the sea from his boyhood to the time when national duty beckoned him to the irksome drudgery of the desk; at the end the sea called him back, and he went to it to return no more. He knew his ships as he knew his child. He knew every plank, every stick, every spar, every cord, from truck to keelson. He loved his ships as he loved his only son. He was one of the most highly skilled navigators of an age when deeds almost miraculous were done with ships little better than cock-boats, when tiny caravels sailed the ocean and pinnaces braved the *furicanos* of the Caribbean Sea. He sailed thousands of leagues in little craft like the *Solomon,* and big ships like the *Jesus of Lubek,* the *Victory,* and the *Garland,* and sailed them equally well. He pushed their noses through waters strange and distant, measuring currents and taking soundings as he went; he brought them masterly through the wildest weather, fought calms and thirst in the Sargasso Sea, and storms in the Western Ocean, weathered the dread *nortes* in the Gulf, and, shorthanded, with exhausted crews, and ships ill-found, coasted the American continent, pierced the fogs of the banks of Newfoundland, and won his way to England again. The nightmare struggle in a morass of figures at the Treasurer's office tortured him into sighs; but on his own quarter-deck he was ever strong, self-reliant, undisturbed, captain of his soul. This was the man who was trusted by his officers and idolised by his mariners; he was never at a loss for an expedient in any situation, however difficult. As John Davis said: [1]

"The first Englishman that gave any attempt on the coasts of West India, being part of America, was Sir John Hawkins, knight, who there and in that attempt, as in many other sithens, did and hath proved himself to be a man of excellent capacity, great government, and perfect resolution. For before he attempted the same it was a matter doubtful, and reported the extremest limit of danger, to sail upon those coasts. So that it was generally in dread among us, such is the slowness of our nation, for the most part of us rather joy at home like epicures to sit and carp at other men's hazards, ourselves not daring to give an attempt. I mean such as are at leisure to seek the good of their country, not being any ways employed as painful members of a common-weal, then either to further or give due commendation to the deservers: how, then, may Sir Hawkins be esteemed, who, being a man of good account in his country, of wealth and great employment, did, notwithstanding, for the good of his country, to procure trade, give that notable and resolute attempt."

This was John Davis, of Sandridge, near Dartmouth, a contemporary of Hawkins, who knew him well, and was highly qualified to speak of Hawkins's services to geographical discovery and the maritime sciences. The Hydrographical Description, "whereby it appears that there is a short and speedy passage into the South Seas, to China, etc., by Northerly Navigation," was published in the year of Hawkins's death; it was in sequel to the accounts of his voyages in search of the North-West passage written by Davis nine years before. No doubt can exist that his opinion of Hawkins's merits was shared by all men in his time, except those whose animosity had been inspired by the Treasurer's ruthless rooting out of jobbery in the departments under his control.

John Hawkins had a great fund of resistance. He was both solid and stolid. He could not be made to comply with an opinion unless he had been fully persuaded of its justice and wisdom. He was slow in forming his own view, but when it had been formed, after a long process of inward balancing of the pros and cons, he could not be moved from it. Thus, in consultation with others, he did not express himself readily, but when the words did come, they were plain, blunt, and decided; if a question remained in doubt, and he could find no solution, he left it for things of which he had certainty. With the quality of resistance, he combined its complement, perfect endurance. He was firm, almost immovable; no hardship could unnerve him. His memory of persons, events, and places was remarkable; he obtained and exercised in this way the full benefits of his great experience. It was this fact that fed his notable faculty of instant choice of the best way out of a tight corner. Slow as he was to speak, he was quick to see and prompt to act in urgent cases.

His shortness of speech gave him sometimes the appearance of boorishness; he did not dissemble, he would not toady. But for his sailors, the men who did his work, his affection was almost unlimited, and did not lack verbal and practical expression. He preserved the strictest authority, but he never tyrannised, and he was always willing to sacrifice himself for his poor mariners. The solicitude he displayed for the men marooned on the coast of Mexico, after the affair of San Juan, was undiminished by the passage of time; he never rested until he had exhausted every effort mortal man could make for their redemption. In many practical ways he laboured to improve the lot of the English seamen, and in the Chatham Chest and in the Hospital he founded he left an enduring monument of his regard for the race among which he had been bred and had spent his youth and prime.

According to his lights, Hawkins was what is described as a God-fearing man. In practice he was a generous Christian — "merciful, apt to forgive, and faithful to his word," as Maynard said. He gave of his substance for charity during his life, and made bequests to the poor in his will. In creed, he was an enthusiastic Protestant. While he fought Philip, he was fighting the Inquisition; his letters are animated by the spirit of hatred and defiance of that evil thing, of which English sailors knew so painfully the terrible power.

Not so brilliant an adventurer as Drake, merely because his activities and his opportunities were not the same; not so great an explorer as Gilbert, or Frobisher, or Cavendish, or Davis, for the same reason; he was, nevertheless, a true representative, as he was one of the pioneers, of the great school of English seamen whose bequest to the nation it is impossible to estimate in any material terms of value.

[1] In "The World's Hydrographical Description."

Notes

A. — The Family of Hawkins

"Hawkyns" was the spelling used by the family until more recent times. The name occurs in the annals of Plymouth as far back as 1480. But intimately as the Hawkinses were associated with the work of the seamen of the West and with the local life of Plymouth, they were not originally a Westcountry breed. They were, in the first place, the Hawkingses of the village of Hawking in the Hundred of Folkestone, so that when in the latter part of Elizabeth's reign John Hawkins was administering the Navy from Deptford, and instituting his charities in the County of Kent, he was working in the very region out of which his ancestors had come. In the reign of Henry II., Osbert de Hawking lived in Kent, and a descendant of his was Andrew Hawkings, of Nash Court, near Faversham, in the time of Edward III. Andrew came into possession of Nash Court by his marriage with the heiress, Joan de Nash. It is from this union that the Hawkinses of Devon are derived. A branch of the family had settled in Plymouth by the middle of the fifteenth century, probably. At any rate, in 1480 a John Hawkins was holding land from the Corporation of the town; he died before 1490, and his heirs continued in possession of the property. Some members of the family migrated to Tavistock, the picturesque town, fifteen miles to the north, clustered round the Abbey, which was then in the full tide of its prosperity and influence. Tavistock has another association interesting for us to remember: it was the birthplace of Francis Drake.

The favourite Christian names in the Hawkins family were William and John. A John Hawkins who had gone to Tavistock married Joan, daughter of William Amadas, of Launceston. He returned to Plymouth towards the end of the fifteenth century, and it is believed that his son William was born there soon after. That son was the first of the three great generations of seamen, and we are now arrived at something like certitude in the matter of dates.

In the year 1513, a William Hawkyns was master of the *Great Galley.* So far as can be ascertained, the only seaman of repute owning that name was William Hawkins, of Plymouth, and it is probable that he and the master of the royal ship were the same person. The *Great Galley* stood second in the list of the men-of-war in King Henry's Navy in the 13th year of his reign, as we find from the details preserved in the Pepys Collection, at Magdalen College, Cambridge. The royal fleet then consisted of sixteen vessels, of which two were rowing barges. The largest of the ships was the *Henry Grâce de Dieu,* stated in the Pepys papers to have been of 1,500 tons burthen, but more probably having a tonnage of about 1,000. The *Great Galley* measured 800 tons, and there was one other ship of the same size, the *Sovereign.* Thus early, more than a century before the death of Richard Hawkins, the Compleat Seaman, in 1622, commenced the connection of the family with the naval service.

B. — Authorities

There are few family records of the Hawkinses until we arrive at the work of Sir John's son, Richard. John Hawkins's life is written in action, and its activities are part of the substructure of British naval history. Something has been done towards the recognition of his part in the stirring drama of the sixteenth century. There are Froude's vividly coloured pictures of the half-national, half-private campaign of the West-country seamen against the naval power of Spain during the years when the family of Hawkins was at its apogee. A valuable basis for the study of Hawkins's life and character as a sea-adventurer, as a naval commander, and as a statesman, has been provided by my friend the late Mr. R. N. Worth, of Plymouth, whose contributions to the fruits of historical research have perhaps only been appraised at their true merit by a few persons in the West of England who recognised the immense ability which he displayed as a historian, and regretted that his talents should be confined so largely to material of a purely local nature, and that his reputation did not assume the national proportions it might have reached under other circumstances. An admirable volume of records of the Hawkins family, by Miss Mary W. S. Hawkins, was printed by private subscription in 1888; this collated a large number of papers relating to Sir John, but it did not attempt a study of the historical significance of the Admiral's life, and was inevitably rather of local and personal than of wider interest.

The author acknowledges with much gratitude the courteous assistance of Miss Hawkins, who has lent the portrait from which the frontispiece of the present volume has been produced.

C. — Hawkins and the Admiralty

The Lansdowne MSS. at the British Museum include a curious document (date 1587) written by a person employed by Sir William Winter to spy on Hawkins at Deptford. The accusations are of peculation and misappropriation in the dockyard, but the evidence is feeble, and the bias is manifest. These "artycles of discovery of the unjust mynde and deceiptfull dealings of Mr. John Hawkins" had so much effect upon the Queen and Government that Hawkins remained in charge of the nation's naval affairs, and the next year was Vice-Admiral of the Fleet against the Armada.